AF361302

POLICY LEARNING FROM CANADA

Reforming Scandinavian Immigration and Integration Policies

TRYGVE UGLAND

Policy Learning from Canada

Reforming Scandinavian Immigration and Integration Policies

UNIVERSITY OF TORONTO PRESS
Toronto Buffalo London

© University of Toronto Press 2018
Toronto Buffalo London
www.utorontopress.com
Printed in the U.S.A.

ISBN 978-1-4875-0319-2

Printed on acid-free, 100% post-consumer recycled paper with vegetable-based inks.

Library and Archives Canada Cataloguing in Publication

Ugland, Trygve, 1969–, author
Policy learning from Canada : reforming Scandinavian immigration and integration policies / Trygve Ugland.

Includes bibliographical references and index.
ISBN 978-1-4875-0319-2 (cloth)

1. Canada – Emigration and immigration – Government policy.   2. Social integration – Government policy – Canada.   3. Scandinavia – Emigration and immigration – Government policy.   4. Social integration – Government policy – Scandinavia.   I. Title.

JV7220.U45 2018   304.8'71   C2017-906715-X

This book has been published with the help of a grant from the Federation for the Humanities and Social Sciences, through the Awards to Scholarly Publications Program, using funds provided by the Social Sciences and Humanities Research Council of Canada.

University of Toronto Press acknowledges the financial assistance to its publishing program of the Canada Council for the Arts and the Ontario Arts Council, an agency of the Government of Ontario.

Contents

Figures and Tables

Preface

Transatlantic relations have been at the centre of my research and teaching interests during the last decade. This book focuses on the relationship between Canada and Scandinavia in the area of immigration and integration policy.

The Social Sciences and Humanities Research Council of Canada (SSHRC) provided a generous grant (Insight Development Grant / 430-2012-0707) to support my research as did the Senate Research Committee at Bishop's University for which I am most appreciative. Further, this book has been published with the help of a grant from the Federation for the Humanities and Social Sciences, through the Awards to Scholarly Publications Program, using funds provided by the Social Sciences and Humanities Research Council of Canada.

I wish to thank Daniel Quinlan at the University of Toronto Press for his ongoing support and encouragement. No one could ask for anything more from an editor. I am also grateful to all the politicians, civil servants, and policy experts in Canada, Denmark, Norway, and Sweden who gave so generously of their time to answer my numerous questions and to provide me with invaluable insights during various research trips between 2010 and 2015. Thanks also to the staff at the Scandinavian embassies in Canada who provided me with much useful information. Daniel Lunderquist at the Swedish Embassy in Ottawa deserves special recognition for his enduring support.

I benefited immensely from my visits and meetings with researchers at the following Scandinavian universities in 2012 and 2013: Aalborg University, University of Copenhagen, and University of Southern Denmark in Odense in Denmark; University of Oslo in Norway; and Malmö University and Uppsala University in Sweden. I am also indebted to the participants at the 20th International Conference of Europeanists in Amsterdam where I presented a paper on this topic in 2013. I realized during the meeting that one paper or an article on the topic would not suffice to fully explain the intricacies of policy learning as it relates to Canada's immigration and integration model vis-à-vis the Scandinavian countries. It became abundantly clear that a book-length manuscript was required to give the subject and its theoretical implications the treatment both deserved. I also received useful feedback on different chapters of this book presented at the Association for the Advancement of Scandinavian Studies in Canada (AASSC) Annual Conference and the European Consortium for Political Research (ECPR) General Conference in 2015 that convinced me to expand my research on the subject and to assess its theoretical outcomes.

I am genuinely grateful to three anonymous scholars who provided constructive suggestions to greatly improve an earlier draft of the manuscript. Thanks to Vebjørn Aalandslid (Statistics Norway) who helped me navigate the complex world of comparative population statistics and the following colleagues who read and offered comments on various sections of the book: Martin Bak Jørgensen (Aalborg University), R. Michael McGregor (Bishop's University), Johan P. Olsen (University of Oslo), and Frode Veggeland (University of Oslo). A particular thank you goes to Andrew F. Johnson who read the manuscript in its entirety. I am also indebted to Jorunn Charlotte Matthiessen, Myriam Plourde, Alexandra Powell, and Jennifer Rooney, senior students at Bishop's University, for providing outstanding research assistance.

As always, I have had all the support I needed from home. Clara, Lea, and Catherine: thank you so much!

Trygve Ugland
Sherbrooke, Canada

PART ONE

Introduction

Scandinavians in Search of Solutions: The Canadian Immigration and Integration Policy Model

This Canadian policy breaks fundamentally with the monolithic nation state ideal: it accepts that people should learn at least two languages and live in at least two cultures. Such a policy should also have chances in European countries that are today confronted with large problems related to immigration. But it is a demanding policy, a policy that cannot progress without conflict. It demands openness and willingness to integrate among immigrant families: it also demands that the majority accept pluralization and view it as a benefit not only for the immigrants but also for the entire society.

Stein Rokkan[1]

Canadian immigration and integration policy has long been held as a potential model for Europe, but its relevance remains largely unexplored. This book remedies this neglect by addressing a fundamental issue of the twenty-first century: policy innovation and learning across state borders, focusing on the relationship between Canada and Scandinavia in the areas of immigration control and immigrant integration policy.

Denmark, Norway, and Sweden have long been portrayed as models for the development of politics and public policies for other states. In his early classic *Sweden: Model for a World* from 1949, American professor Hudson Strode praised the Scandinavian political system as an ideal to strive for, concluding that "the only serious flaw in the happy state of well-ordered Scandinavia is her geographic nearness to Russia."[2] Be that as it may, Scandinavia sustained and enhanced its policies, uniquely distinguished by generous investments in social capital, long after Strode wrote. In 2013, *The Economist* magazine featured a bearded, overweight, horned-helmet-wearing Viking on its front cover, accompanied by the headline, "The Next Supermodel." The overriding message was that "politicians from both left and right can learn" from the Scandinavian countries.[3]

The idea of a Scandinavian model started to gain prominence internationally subsequent to the Great Depression. The relatively swift recovery of the Scandinavian economies was striking, especially given that their recoveries were orchestrated by open parliamentary democracies, and not totalitarian dictatorships like several of their powerful European neighbours.[4] In particular, Marquis Childs's international bestseller of 1936, *Sweden: The Middle Way*, is associated with the discovery of and reference to Scandinavia as an international political and economic model.[5] Despite important national variations, the Scandinavian model is a unique version of the mixed economy because it includes a particularly strong commitment to the welfare state.[6] The international fascination with the Scandinavian model derives from a broadly shared impression that Denmark, Norway, and Sweden have successfully managed to combine private capitalism and the quest for economic growth, on the one hand, with state intervention and the promotion of social equity on the other. Moreover, international observers have noted that the objectives of economic efficiency and social welfare in Scandinavia have reinforced each other as demonstrated by the three Scandinavian countries' consistently high rankings in international indices of competitiveness as well as of happiness.[7] A solid tradition of political pragmatism and societal compromise, together with widespread domestic support for the model, has further contributed to the model's international attraction.[8]

According to Strode, leaders and ordinary citizens of any nation would "profit by examining the agreeable Scandinavian compromise between capitalism and socialism to see what might prove to be constructive blessings to themselves."[9] Apparently, this advice has been widely accepted inasmuch as the Scandinavian model has informed political and academic discourse in many countries. Notably, the Scottish independence movement exemplified the Scandinavian attraction to the fullest. The 2013 white paper on the future for an independent Scotland is generously sprinkled with references to the Scandinavian countries. Denmark, Norway, and Sweden are altogether mentioned more than a hundred times. According to the Scottish government, the Scandinavian countries have demonstrated that "fairness and prosperity are part of a virtuous cycle, reinforcing each other and delivering a range of benefits for society as a whole."[10] Published on the eve of the Scottish referendum in 2014, the book *Small Nations in a Big World: What*

Scotland Can Learn? has a strong focus on the achievements of Scandinavian countries.[11]

The Scandinavian model has also received substantial attention in Canada. Henry Milner's essay, with its self-explanatory title "The Prospects for Scandinavian-Style Social Democracy in Quebec/Canada," represents an early illustration.[12] Even if Milner is less than optimistic about these prospects, Canadian public policy debates have remained saturated with positive references to Scandinavian policies. Canadian academics, journalists, politicians, and leaders of non-governmental organizations alike continue to evoke Scandinavian solutions for Canadian as well as for global challenges. Deliberations on electoral systems (proportional representation), government formation (coalition governments), political and economic representation (gender equality), political participation (voter turnout and tripartite arrangements), political priorities (education, environment, and energy policies), welfare provisions and health-care delivery (private vs. public solutions; free access vs. user fees), and international activism and engagement (humanitarianism and conflict resolution) represent some of the prevailing examples.[13] More recently, the heated battle over the proposed university tuition hikes in Quebec during the spring and summer of 2012, and the latest debate on reform of Canadian prostitution laws, contained many references to Scandinavian systems for higher education and criminal justice, respectively. The common thread in such debates is that Canada could learn worthwhile lessons from Scandinavia.

Although Canada and the world continue to enthuse about the Scandinavian model, questions have been raised about its future. Even the glowing international reputation and the robust moral authority of Scandinavian countries in world politics have recently been cast in doubt.[14] More often than not, the concerns are associated with challenges posed by increased immigration and ethnic diversity.

A Scandinavian Challenge

"Scandinavia" is herein used to refer to the three Scandinavian nation states of Denmark, Norway, and Sweden. Finland and Iceland are not included, although both have overlapping histories and long-standing social and cultural ties and countless similarities with the three Scandinavian states. Because Finnish and Icelandic politics and public policies resemble those of Denmark, Norway, and Sweden in most areas, Finland and Iceland are often included in studies of the Scandinavian political model. In the Scandinavian languages, the concept of "the Nordic Model" (den Nordiske modell) typically refers to all five countries.[15] In the area of immigration and integration policy, however, Finnish and Icelandic realities are distinctively different from Danish, Norwegian, and Swedish experiences. Finland and Iceland became net receivers of immigrants later than did the other three, and their foreign-born populations are still notably lower in numbers than those in Denmark, Norway, and Sweden. The fact that Danish, Norwegian, and Swedish are mutually intelligible while most Finns and Icelanders speak languages that are very different from those spoken by their Scandinavian kin provides a practical reason – and, above all, a convenient one – to simply focus on Denmark, Norway, and Sweden.

The Scandinavian countries of Denmark, Norway, and Sweden share a common history in migration. They can all be described as latecomers to modern immigration. Instead, massive emigration was for long the dominant trend for poor Scandinavians in search of better living circumstances. This is especially true of Norway and Sweden where industrialization began later than in Denmark. The waves of emigration from Norway and Sweden started in the 1840s and lasted until the 1920s, reaching their peak in the 1880s when more than 1 per cent of the population from both countries emigrated annually.[16] Most migrants chose the United States as their end destination, but many Scandinavians also chose Canada. In fact, the Canadian government allocated resources to encourage Scandinavian emigration to Canada during the nineteenth and early twentieth centuries. Reduced ocean-passage rates, free rail transportation to Winnipeg, and land reserves for colonization were some of the measures used.[17] A pioneer of the Canadian social democratic movement, the late J.S. Woodsworth, explains in his 1909 book why the Canadian government offered such incentives: "Taken all in all, there is no class of immigrants that are as certain of making their way in the Canadian West as the people of the peninsula of Scandinavia. Accustomed to the rigours of a northern climate, clean-blooded, thrifty, ambitious and hard working, they will be certain of success in this pioneer country, where the strong, not the weak, are wanted."[18] Woodsworth's oblique references to notions of racial superiority and suitability to Canada were by no means uncommon at the time. In fact, such views were formally embraced in Canada's immigration policies and legislation in the early twentieth century.

Apart from intra-Scandinavian and intra-Nordic migration, immigration to the Scandinavian countries was historically very limited.

Figure 1. Immigration to Denmark, Norway, and Sweden, 1968–2015, absolute numbers

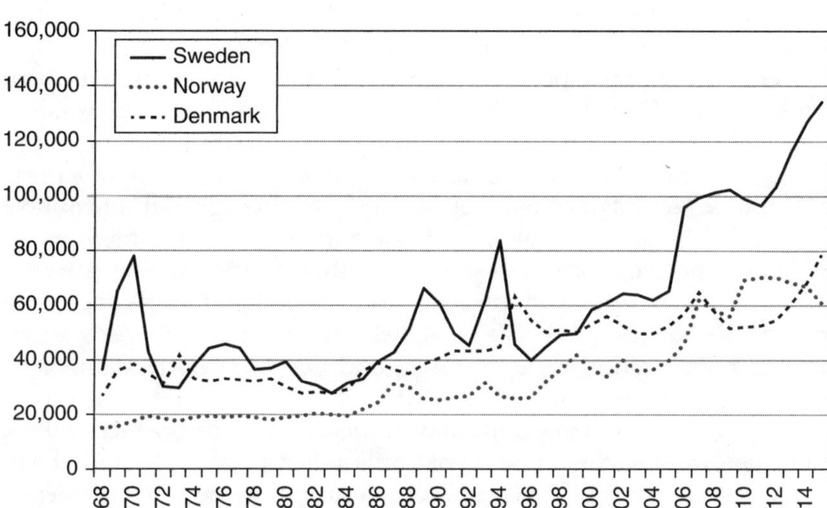

Sources: Statistics Norway; Statistics Sweden; Statistics Denmark; Eurostat.
The figures from 1968 to 2011 are taken from Silje Vatne Pettersen and Lars Østby,
"Skandinavisk komparativ statistikk om integrering: innvandrere i Norge, Sverige og
Danmark," *Samfunnsspeilet*, no. 5 (2013): 76–82.

Sweden first began receiving significant numbers of immigrants during the 1950s, while Denmark and Norway did not become net recipients of migrants until the late 1960s. Since then, the immigrant population has increased steadily in all three countries (Figure 1).

Labour immigration comprised a considerable proportion of total immigration to Denmark, Norway, and Sweden in the early post-war years as substantial numbers of predominantly male migrant workers arrived in response to job opportunities in the private sector.[19] However, Sweden, Denmark, and Norway effectively abandoned their open immigration policies in 1972, 1973, and 1975, respectively, due to economic recession and to concomitant high unemployment.[20] Despite the restrictions on labour immigration, the three countries continued to pursue relatively liberal policies towards refugees during the 1970s and 1980s. After a modest growth, the number of asylum seekers and refugees rose rapidly from the early 1990s due to the emergence of a number of new international conflicts in Europe and elsewhere. There was also a steady increase in the number of immigrants joining family members who were already established in Denmark, Norway, and Sweden; these immigrants were accepted under the family reunification regulations of this period. Figure 1 illustrates that up until the turn of the century, Denmark had almost as many immigrants as Sweden. Since 2000, however, Sweden has received far more immigrants per year compared with both Denmark and Norway.

Denmark, Norway, and Sweden have officially recognized "old minorities" and indigenous peoples, but these populations have amounted to less than 1 per cent of the overall population in the three countries.[21] Denmark's minorities include Faroe Islanders, Germans, Greenlanders, and Roma. The Kven, Jews, Forest Finns, and Roma are recognized national minorities in Norway, and the Sami are recognized as an indigenous people. Sweden's official minorities include Jews, Roma, Romani, Sami, Swedish Finns, and Tornedalers. Because these ethnic minorities were subject to strict assimilationist policies, Scandinavian countries prior to World War II were depicted as the most ethnically homogeneous countries in Europe.[22] However, recent immigration has changed this. For the first time, the Scandinavian nations have a noticeably diverse population in terms of ethnicity, at least in the major urban centres. The immigrant population in Denmark, Norway, and Sweden is currently around 9, 13, and 17 per cent, respectively (Figure 2).

The sheer number of immigrants, as well as the composition of this population with respect to countries of origin, has varied over time. The immigrant population has also varied between Denmark, Norway, and Sweden. Sweden currently has about three times as many immigrants as Norway and Denmark (1.7 million vs. 0.7 and 0.5 million). About half of all immigrants in Scandinavia are from countries in Asia, Africa, or Latin America.[23] The early immigrants were mainly migrant workers, followed by refugees and the families of these two groups. The next-largest group of immigrants is from European Union countries outside the Nordic region and is currently dominated by labour immigrants from Eastern Europe. Immigrants from the Nordic countries make up the third-largest group in Norway and Sweden. Disregarding the sizeable intra-Scandinavian migration (for instance, the high number of Swedes currently in Norway), non-Western immigrants from countries such as Iraq, Iran, Pakistan, the Philippines, Somalia, Sudan, Syria, Turkey, Vietnam, and the former Yugoslavia are today among the largest immigrant groups in Scandinavia. Although the general picture

Figure 2. Population composition in Denmark, Norway, and Sweden,*
1 January 2016, per cent

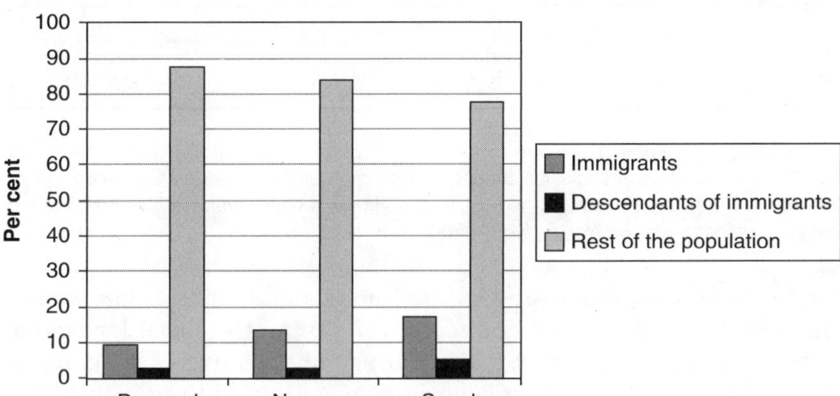

* Foreign-born persons in Sweden.
Sources: Statistics Norway; Statistics Sweden; Statistics Denmark.

is relatively similar for the three Scandinavian countries, there are differences when examining the number of immigrants from different countries of origin. However, the number of immigrants from Syria has increased significantly in all three countries since 2014.

The post-war shift from ethnic homogeneity to ethnic pluralism and multicultural diversity has raised issues that have become sources of tension and politicization in Scandinavia. The future of the welfare state has been a central theme.[24] The notion that there is a potential trade-off between an open and accommodating approach to immigration and the maintenance of a robust welfare state has been increasingly expressed in many European countries.[25] The universalistic and generous Scandinavian welfare model has been regarded as particularly vulnerable. Brochmann makes the point succinctly: "Immigration to a country that espouses the principle of equal treatment and has an extensive welfare state challenges the population's generosity in the first instance, and *may* in the longer term affect the sustainability of the system itself if the bulk of the newcomers are unable to support themselves ... Good welfare states do not tolerate substantial elements of persons or groups that fall by the wayside, that disturb the regulated world of work and burden social welfare budgets."[26]

Table 1. Shares in employment for ages 25–64 in Denmark, Norway, and Sweden in 2011, per cent

	Denmark	Norway	Sweden
Entire population	74.4	79.9	78.5
Immigrants*	54.6	67.9	57.0

* Foreign-born persons in Sweden.
Sources: Labour market statistics: Statistics Norway; Statistics Sweden; Statistics Denmark; Silje Vatne Pettersen and Lars Østby, *Skandinavisk komparativ statistikk om integrering: innvandrere i Norge, Sverige og Danmark.*

Because the Scandinavian welfare state generally rejects targeted or means-tested welfare services, while promoting the social incorporation of immigrants through universal benefits, its future depends on workforce participation from all groups of society. However, there has been a growing awareness that the efforts to integrate immigrants into the workforce have not succeeded in Scandinavia. Organisation for Economic Co-operation and Development (OECD) data, for instance, demonstrate that the Scandinavian countries fare poorly compared with many other countries in integrating immigrants into the labour market. Unemployment rates are significant higher for foreign-born men and women than for native-born persons.[27] Table 1 gives an overview of the employment situation for immigrants in the three Scandinavian countries for 2011.

The significant immigrant-native employment gap in the Scandinavian countries is a central concern with direct links to the future of the welfare state. Although there is little evidence to support the contention that increasing ethnic diversity *as such* has adverse effects on established welfare states,[28] a growing chorus of commentators has argued that ethnic/racial diversity may make it more difficult to sustain redistributive policies in the long run. In the Scandinavian context, it has, for instance, been emphasized that social homogeneity, in terms of ethnicity, language, and religion, was the source of the values of solidarity, reciprocity, and, above all, the social equity that supported the Scandinavian welfare model.[29] The future of this model has, therefore, been linked to the existence of a society-wide understanding of belonging. Thus according to Ingebritsen: "If divisions emerge over 'we' versus 'them,' and the culture is unable to redefine its traditions and day-to-day practices to accommodate differences and translate them into membership, the model of Scandinavian welfare is at risk."[30] In this respect, the Scandinavian countries are facing new challenges: "A form of belonging is needed within which one can live out one's diversity – some sort of 'we' – even though considerably altered. In this respect, no happy moment has arrived in any of the Nordic countries."[31]

In lieu of this "happy moment," immigration has become a target for increasingly popular right-wing populist political parties in all three Scandinavian countries, and recently anti-immigration statements have also been made through illegitimate political activities, even by means of extreme violence. On 22 July 2011, the Norwegian right-wing fanatic, Anders Behring Breivik, killed seventy-seven people ostensibly to defend Norway and Europe against multiculturalism. Earlier, the Danish Muhammad cartoon controversy of 2005 and 2006, and the serious riots in several Swedish cities during the summer of 2013 both reflected and triggered increasingly strained relations between native Scandinavians and various immigrant communities. While most ethnic Danes defended the Danish newspaper's right to publish satirical cartoons of the Prophet Muhammad, many Muslims in Denmark, as well as abroad, vehemently protested against the publications. Likewise, many perceive the recent Swedish riots as a reflection of the growing gap in employment and living conditions between natives and recent immigrants to Sweden. Although different in many ways, these events do not correspond to the customary image of a peaceful and harmonious Scandinavia, idealized by Hudson Strode almost seventy years ago.[32]

Although popular opinion towards immigrants among the majority populations in Denmark, Norway, and Sweden during the 2000s tended to be far more positive than the oft-heated debates among media pundits would have it, sizeable proportions of the surveyed populations agree or strongly agree with expressions of negative sentiments towards immigrants. However, there are significant differences in attitudes among the Scandinavian countries. According to Yngve Lithman, Sweden is consistently the most liberal in terms of attitudes towards immigrants. Denmark is the least liberal, and Norway is somewhere in-between.[33] Political parties with anti-immigration agendas have also, until very recently, enjoyed more success in Denmark and Norway than in Sweden. However, the last general election in Sweden in 2014, when the right-wing Sweden Democrats polled 12.9 per cent of the popular vote and won 14 per cent of the seats in Parliament, indicates that intra-Scandinavian differences have narrowed.

The current challenges that the Scandinavian countries are facing have attracted attention elsewhere, including in Canada. In a recent

Canadian study of multiculturalism, for instance, Denmark is exposed as the archetype of the international multiculturalism villain.[34] In his essay, John Ibbitson even seems obliged to warn immigrants about seeking their fortune in Denmark:

> Copenhagen is a beautiful city, and Danish culture is rich. But our Filipino engineer will face considerable challenges if she moves there. First, she will have to learn Danish, one of the many European languages that has little currency outside of its own borders. She will also have to accept that she will never truly be Danish. To be a Dane is to be the inheritor of centuries of history and cultural development. Danes act Danish, look Danish, think Danish. It isn't easy to be a Filipino-Dane. It may not be easy to be the grandchild of a Filipino-Dane.[35]

In a tongue-in-cheek comment, the popular American novelist, Richard Ford, remarks that the situation is vastly different for immigrants to Canada because "it's not hard to be a Canadian. Kenyans and Indians and Germans do it with ease."[36]

A Canadian Model

Although the domestic circumstances differ, the public debate on immigration and integration reforms has intensified in Denmark, Norway, and Sweden during the past two decades. In this reform process, the Scandinavian countries have searched for inspiration and new policy solutions abroad. Although many countries and models have been given attention, this book focuses on the specific role that the Canadian immigration and integration policy model has played in the Scandinavian reform process from 2000 to 2015, its so-called reassessment phase.[37]

The challenges posed by increasing immigration and ethnocultural diversity are major concerns for governments across the world. Different immigration and integration policy solutions exist internationally. Canada has pursued an expansive immigration policy for an extensive period of time, and its immigrant population has grown substantially (Figure 3). For the past twenty-five years, Canada has received between 200,000 and 300,000 immigrants per year, representing on average just under 1 per cent of the population. Canada has one of the highest levels of foreign-born populations (approximately 20 per cent, according to the OECD) and is one of the most multicultural countries in the world.[38]

Figure 3. Immigration to Canada, 1860–2015, absolute numbers

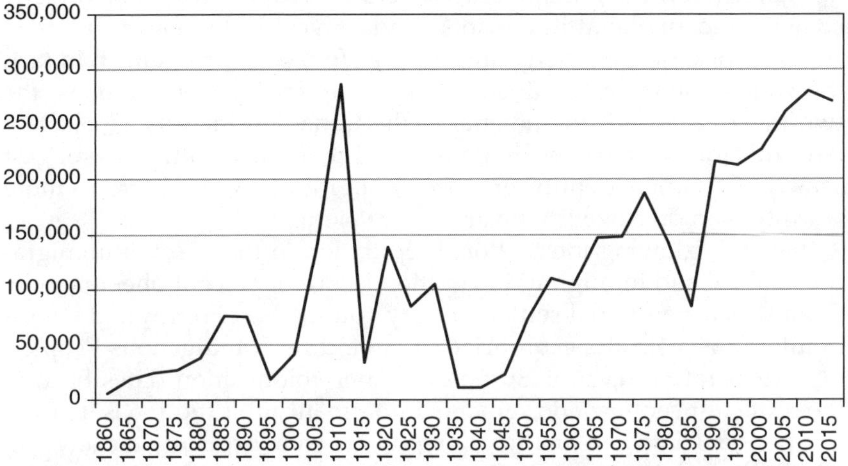

Source: Government of Canada, "Facts and Figures 2015: Immigration Overview – Permanent Residents." Ottawa: Immigration, Refugees and Citizenship Canada, 2016.

At the same time, Canada enjoys a strong international reputation, supported by comparative studies on immigrant integration, as a country that has successfully managed to benefit from increased ethnocultural diversity. In fact, Canada has been described as a "statistical outlier" in that it has managed to combine high levels of diversity with peace, democracy, economic prosperity, and individual freedom.[39] Furthermore, Canada has managed to reconcile important welfare-state objectives and principles with increased immigration and diversity. While the Scandinavian countries distribute services to new immigrants not just according to expressed needs, but according to principles of universality, Canada's welfare policy is more residual and without the same commitment to equality of outcome.[40] Also, more emphasis is put on initiatives from the newcomers themselves in order to integrate successfully into the Canadian labour market and society compared with the expectations that newcomers to Denmark, Norway, and Sweden have traditionally been met with. Although not as universal, comprehensive, and generous as the Scandinavian welfare states, the Canadian social security system includes unemployment insurance, child tax credits, universal childcare benefits, medicare, the Canada Pension Plan, old age security, social assistance, and a host of other socially oriented tax deductions and tax credits. In contrast to many other countries, Canada has not actively sought to restrict access to welfare provisions to newcomers, and public attitudes in Canada reveal little tension between support for ethnic diversity and support for social programs.[41] In fact, the welfare state and multiculturalism are, for many Canadians, the two most important ingredients in the Canadian identity. Consistent with this impression, research has found that those with the strongest sense of Canadian identity embrace immigration and immigrants more warmly than do citizens who are less patriotic.[42]

Canada's glowing international reputation in the areas of immigration control and immigrant integration is a rather recent phenomenon. Canada is a traditional settler country, founded on French and British immigration with the expropriation of land from Indigenous Peoples. The deliberate project of European settler colonization dates back to the sixteenth century and remained dominant until the 1960s. During this period, Canadian immigration policies were explicitly racially and ethnically discriminatory. Approximately 90 per cent of all immigrants to Canada came from Europe in this period. However, between 1961 and 1996, only 19 per cent came from European countries with 57 per cent coming from countries in Asia.[43] This shift has been reflected in the growing number of visible minorities in Canada, defined by Statistics Canada as "persons who are non-Caucasian in race or non-white in colour and who do not report being Aboriginal."[44] According to the 2011 Census, visible minorities represented 19.1 per cent of the population.[45] This is up from 6.3 per cent in 1986. During the 2006–11 period, almost 60 per cent of the immigrants who arrived in Canada came from Asia (including the Middle East). In contrast, immigrants from Asia accounted for less than 10 per cent prior to the 1970s.[46] This development is a result of changes in public policies. The most significant change has been the introduction of a new immigration and integration policy model in the 1960s and 1970s.

The new Canadian approach to immigration control and immigrant integration has been characterized by different labels: "the Canadian model of pluralism";[47] "the Canadian model of multiculturalism";[48] "the Canadian model of multicultural integration";[49] "the Canadian model of diversity";[50] "the Canadian model of immigration and welfare";[51] "the Canadian immigration model";[52] "the Canadian integration model";[53] and "Canada's immigration policy model."[54]

The construction and application of "national models" have contributed significantly to the field of comparative migration research over the past decades.[55] For instance, these models have been used as analytical lenses to highlight distinct differences between countries, but also to expose variations within single countries over time. Despite the advantages of comparison, models provide only a "simplified picture of a part of the real world."[56] The wide assortment of labels applied to the Canadian case demonstrates the inherent simplification that "national modelling" involves as scholars focus on different features of a complex empirical reality. In this book, the concept of the *Canadian immigration and integration policy model* is employed to include both the Canadian policies regulating the control of the influx of immigrants (immigration policy) and the policies governing how immigrants are treated once they have entered the country (integration policy). As will be further problematized and discussed, ideas and concepts of national models, and the Canadian immigration and integration policy model in particular, are not institutionally consistent, normatively coherent, culturally defined, or historically stable. Instead, these models – including the Canadian immigration and integration policy model – will be considered as complex structures of reference.[57]

Both immigration control and immigrant integration are areas of shared jurisdiction between the federal and provincial governments in Canada, and although provincial governments are playing increasingly important roles, the Canadian immigration and integration policy model can be approached by identifying two main characteristics. First, and with respect to immigration control, Canada abandoned explicit policies of racial and ethnic discrimination in 1967, and instead adopted a new system of evaluation to assess all immigrants according to the same criteria. In this new selective and carefully managed approach to immigration control, priority was on attracting economic immigrants. The economic-class stream has dominated since the 1990s. Currently, this group, including spouses and dependents, constitutes nearly two-thirds of immigrants arriving in Canada annually. The family stream comprises approximately 25 per cent, while refugees represent approximately 15 per cent of immigrants coming to Canada each year (Figure 4).

The "points" and "sponsorship" systems are key components of the Canadian model. Economic immigrants are selected through a points system that grants priority to those most likely to be able to enter the Canadian labour force by virtue of their age, education, work experience, language skills, and adaptability. Successful applicants require a minimum of 67 out of 100 points, where a maximum of 28 points is given

Figure 4. Permanent residents to Canada by category per year, absolute numbers

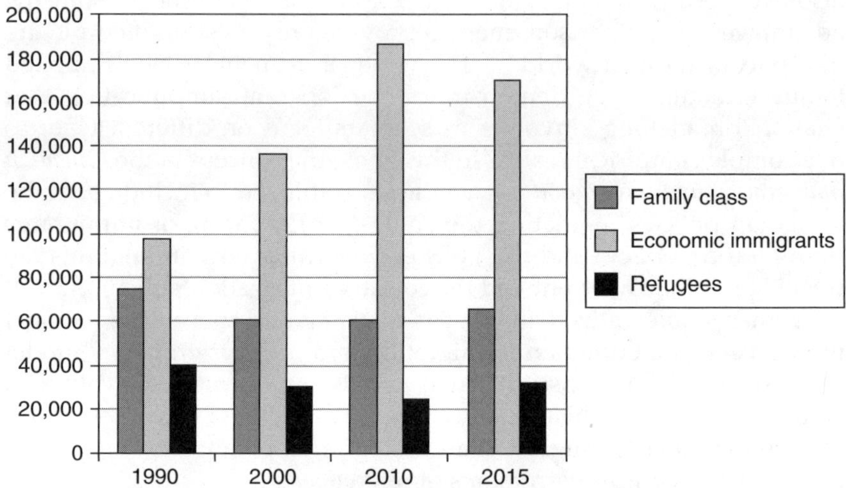

Source: Government of Canada, "Facts and Figures 2015: Immigration Overview – Permanent Residents." Ottawa: Immigration, Refugees and Citizenship Canada, 2016.

for language proficiency in English and/or French; 25 points for educational attainment; 15 for work experience; 12 for age; 10 for arranged employment; and, finally, 10 for a characteristic called "adaptability." Family immigrants seeking to enter Canada to be reunited with their families require sponsors committed to supporting them economically for a significant period of time. Persons eligible for sponsorship include dependent children, spouses, parents, and grandparents. Sponsored family-class immigrants are normally not eligible for social assistance for the duration of the sponsorship period.

Canada also makes extensive use of private sponsorships in order to provide financial and emotional support for refugees. Local, regional, or national religious organizations, ethnocultural groups, and humanitarian organizations most commonly provide private sponsorship for refugees. According to the Canadian government, sponsoring groups agree to provide the refugees with care, lodging, settlement assistance, and support for the duration of the sponsorship period – normally twelve months starting from the refugee's arrival in Canada or until the refugee becomes self-sufficient, whichever comes first.[58] Private sponsors typically support refugees by covering the cost of food, rent, household utilities, and other day-to-day living expenses; providing clothing, furniture, and other household goods; locating interpreters; selecting a family physician and dentist; assisting with applying for provincial health-care coverage; enrolling children in school and adults in language training; introducing newcomers to people with similar personal interests; providing orientation with regard to banking services, transportation, and the like; and helping in the search for employment.

Second, Canada's multiculturalist citizenship represents an important element in its approach to immigrant integration. Multiculturalism refers to a policy that recognizes diversity within public institutions and celebrates it as an important dimension of collective life and collective identity.[59] While integration and multiculturalism are sometimes portrayed as opposed to each other, multiculturalism is used as an instrument of integration in Canada. Canadians are, therefore, both multiculturalists and integrationists.[60] Multiculturalism as a policy attaches positive value to cultural diversity and therefore actively aims to support the various cultures. Spurred by concerns for minority rights, in particular the rights of Indigenous Peoples and the special status of Quebec, Canada began to turn away from its assimilationist policies of the past in the 1960s. This change was accelerated after Canada became the first country in the world to adopt an official public policy of recognizing and accommodating ethnocultural diversity, sanctioned by a parliamentary statement in 1971. The policy was enshrined in the Canadian Multiculturalism Act of 1988 and given constitutional recognition in section 27 of the Constitution.

Canada has followed up on this constitutional commitment by adopting the world's most robust multicultural policies, according to the internationally recognized Multiculturalism Policy Index.[61] Programs supported under Canada's multiculturalism policy, to mention a few, include the allowance of dual citizenship; antiracism campaigns and programs on how to improve ethnic representation and cultural sensitivity in schools, health-care institutions, police, and the media; inclusion of multiculturalism in school curricula and academic studies of the history of ethnic groups in Canada; public funding for ethnic-group organizations and activities such as ethnic festivals; and exemptions from dress codes in certain areas. The exemption from dress codes was sanctioned, with pervasive implications, by the solicitor general's directive in 1990 that Sikhs could wear turbans as part of the iconic uniform of the Royal Canadian Mounted Police (RCMP). All in all, the Canadian multiculturalist approach is built on a conception of integration that holds that immigrants will visibly and proudly express their ethnic identity, and that accepts an obligation on the part of public institutions to accommodate ethnic identities.[62] As an instrument of immigrant integration, Canada's multiculturalism policy permits dual citizenship and aims to rapidly transform newcomers into citizens. For instance, permanent residents may apply for citizenship after only three years of residency. In addition to measures directly earmarked for the immigrant population, indirect integration policy measures exist in the form of general welfare policies. Immigrants have, with few exceptions, immediate and undifferentiated access to social benefits and are not restricted by long residency requirements.[63] In addition to government-funded services for immigrants, a vast number of private charities and non-profit groups are actively involved in the integration process.

By contrast to many other countries, Canadian immigration and integration policies are supported by an overwhelming political consensus at the federal level.[64] All of Canada's main political parties agree with the comparatively high admission totals of immigrants annually, and official multiculturalism continues to enjoy the backing of Canadian governments, regardless of ideological orientation.[65] There is rarely any debate about immigration during Canadian election campaigns.[66] In fact, federal immigration and integration policy has been described as "de-politicized" due to what has been referred to as a "liberal and expansionary consensus."[67] Opinion polls since the early 2000s confirm this consensus: between 60 and 70 per cent of the Canadian population either systematically supports current immigration levels or wants them increased.[68] The international attraction of the Canadian model is to a large extent based on the domestic consensus over immigration and integration policy.

According to Jeffrey G. Reitz, the most significant distinctive feature of the Canadian approach is "the belief that immigration represents a positive opportunity to build the economy and develop the country."[69] However, with clear links to the wider issue of migration and the welfare state, the deeply entwined relationship between the policies on immigration control and immigrant integration is in this book seen as the main defining feature of the Canadian model. While the comprehensive programs that new immigrants can rely on are likely to have an independent effect on immigrant integration, Canada's selective and carefully managed immigration strategy is also aimed at maximizing

Figure 5. The Canadian immigration and integration policy model

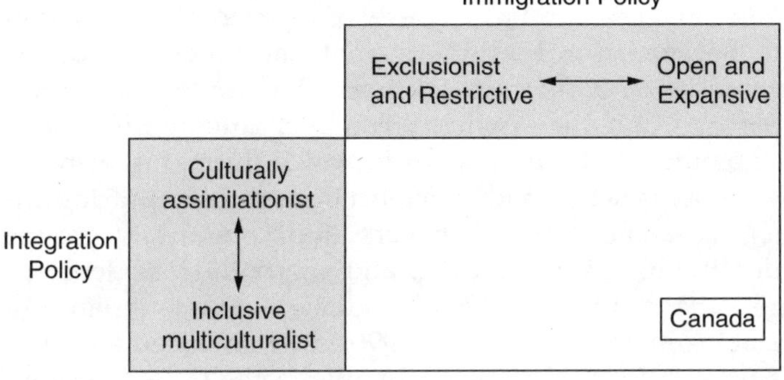

integration and minimizing immigrants' reliance on state support and the welfare budgets. Research has demonstrated that skilled labour immigrants to Canada in fact integrate more easily in the labour market than assisted relatives and refugees.[70] In turn, the successful integration of immigrants makes it possible to welcome a high number of immigrants to the country every year. The relationship between immigration control and immigrant integration is also recognized institutionally: the same government ministry, Citizenship and Immigration Canada (CIC), is responsible for both efforts.[71] Although the Canadian model could be defined by separate references to either its open and expansionary immigration policies or its inclusive multicultural integration policies, it is the deeply entwined relationship between the two that constitutes the real core of the model. Canada first promotes diversity and integration through liberal and carefully managed immigration policies, and then celebrates diversity through multicultural integration policies.

The deeply entwined and carefully managed relationship between immigration control and immigrant integration is of utmost importance to bear in mind when studying how the Canadian model is used internationally and most particularly in Scandinavia. On the continuums of immigration and integration policies, Figure 5 illustrates that Canada is comfortably positioned in the "open and expansive" and "inclusive multiculturalist" corner, and has been so since the 1970s. The locations of Denmark, Norway, and Sweden, however, have varied considerably during the same time period. As the country case studies will demonstrate in more detail, there are also significant differences among the three Scandinavian countries today.

The Canadian government has actively promoted the Canadian model abroad. For instance, the government has funded academic research, conferences, and policy workshops that explore the international relevance of Canadian policies. The international Metropolis Project is perhaps the most well known initiative through which the Canadian government has provided financial incentives and logistical support for researchers, policy-makers, and community groups engaged in identifying, understanding, and responding to developments in migration and diversity. The Canadian government played a vital role in establishing the network in 1996, and performed a leadership role in it until 2012. According to Kymlicka, the Canadian government used its leadership role to ensure that the accommodation of immigrant diversity through "Canadian style multiculturalism" was one of the major research areas of the network.[72] The Canadian influence was also visible in a number of other ways. For instance, Ottawa was one of two cities providing the permanent secretariat for the Metropolis Project with a federal government official, Howard Duncan, as the executive head. When the federal government ceased funding the Metropolis Project in 2012, its secretariat was transferred from the Government of Canada to Carleton University in the Canadian capital. Howard Duncan continued in his role as executive head, but now from his office and as an employee of Carleton University. By 2015, Metropolis had a global network of sixty-eight partner organizations – composed of universities, think tanks, governments, service-providing agencies, and international organizations – in twenty-three countries. The Canadian model has also historically been promoted internationally by the Canadian government through the activities of the Forum of Federations, the International Council for Canadian Studies, and various government agencies, as well as through the day-to-day work of Canadian embassies worldwide.[73]

The link between policy-makers on the one hand, and academic researchers and scientific experts on the other, is closely associated with the genesis and diffusion of the Canadian model. Several of the world's leading theorists and scholars of multiculturalism are, in fact, Canadian: Will Kymlicka and Charles Taylor being perhaps the two most prominent examples.[74] Kymlicka – who in all openness admits that his own work has been supported by all of the above organizations[75] – cites three reasons why the Canadian model is promoted internationally.[76]

First, there may be humanitarian motives, based on the belief that other countries will benefit from studying the Canadian model. Second, a self-interested interpretation posits that international promotion may help to foster an image of Canada as "diversity friendly" and an attractive place to visit, to do business with, or even to live in. Third, international initiatives may serve the purpose of legitimizing Canadian policies domestically. Selling the Canadian model to foreigners can, according to Kymlicka, indirectly help sell it to Canadians. Domestic critics of Canadian immigration and integration policies will have a hard time if the rest of the world declares the Canadian model a success. A fourth reason can be added to this list of motives behind the international marketing of the Canadian model: "policy learning" holds that Canada can be expected to learn from exchanges on policy experiences with other countries. These exchanges can be an important source of refinement and improvement for the Canadian immigration and integration policy model.

Despite extensive promotional efforts, very little systematic attention has been paid to investigating whether and how the Canadian model has been used internationally to address challenges posed by increased immigration and ethnic diversity. However, there is an abundance of anecdotal evidence suggesting that both foreign countries and international organizations have expressed interest in Canada's experiences. Apparent interest in Canada's approach to diversity have, for instance, been indicated by a Japanese ambassador to Canada, parliamentarians from the Ivory Coast, and the UNESCO World Commission on Culture and Development.[77] Also, German politicians are alleged to have routinely travelled to Canada to learn about the Canadian model during the past decade.[78]

Although some policy advocates seem to recommend and promote the Canadian model to foreign audiences without even questioning its exportability or international relevance, others regard the Canadian model as a product of unique and favourable domestic circumstances that make it ill-suited for other countries lacking similar underlying conditions.[79] Kymlicka, for instance, suggests that the precise timing of the introduction of multiculturalism, and Canada's unique geography, limit the exportability of the Canadian model to other nations.[80] Nevertheless, based on the literature on policy transfer,[81] a basic premise advanced here is that policy-makers *can* learn from their observations of policies and programs even in foreign systems.

Sometimes countries also draw negative lessons from abroad. For instance, despite their overall reputation, Canadian policies have sometimes received international criticism from a global social justice perspective because Canada attracts and selects highly educated and skilled workers from poorer countries.[82] Outflow of skilled migrants from developing to developed countries, the so-called brain drain, can create hardship and seriously hamper the development of the former. Also, Canada's Temporary Foreign Worker Program has been criticized on a number of accounts. The key criticism is that temporary foreign labour migrants are particularly vulnerable to exploitation compared with high-skilled immigrants, who in most cases are able to attain Canadian citizenship relatively quickly.[83] Canada has also been criticized for its treatment of its own Indigenous populations who, in many areas, remain politically and socially marginalized.[84]

Multiculturalism also has its critics in Canada and elsewhere. For some, Canadian multiculturalism is seen as a destructive force that promotes ghettos and cultural isolation among groups rather than integration. Unreasonable accommodation offered to different cultural practices, resulting in moral relativism, is another concern. Similarly, equality rights and multiculturalism are sometimes said to be uneasy partners. Neil Bissoondath's book *Selling Illusions* has provided the most influential critique of multiculturalism in Canada.[85] The criticism by Bissoondath and others, in turn, has been met by voices accusing the critics of suffering from the "diffuse anxiety" of *multicultiphobia*.[86] The argument advanced is that the criticism contains significant logical flaws and that contradictory ills are attributed to multiculturalism. The debate is not over, and frictions and tensions related to multiculturalism in Canada continue to be dealt with in a context of routine politics with reference to established case law and the Canadian Charter of Rights and Freedoms. Certainly, it is difficult to speak about a major Canadian backlash against or retreat from multiculturalism, European style.[87] According to a 2014 poll, 65 per cent of Canadians agreed with the following statement: "I am proud of Canada's multicultural makeup."[88] Only 12 per cent disagreed with the statement.

However, there are regional differences in the attitudes towards multiculturalism. For instance, Quebecers worry more than other Canadians that their own cultural values are threatened by increased ethnic diversity.[89] In particular, many francophone Quebecers sense that multiculturalism has negated the principle of dualism on which Canada was founded: two founding peoples and two nations.[90] Charging that multiculturalism fails to recognize the special status of the francophone community, Quebec has actively tried to distance itself from the

Canadian model by constructing its own approach to immigrant integration: "interculturalism." This approach seeks to assert the primacy of Quebec in politics, culture, and identity, understood in the context of a larger project of affirming the Quebec nation.[91] The central idea is that immigrants and minority cultures are invited to integrate into the larger host community of francophone Quebec. To accomplish this objective and to facilitate integration, Quebec – which established its own ministry of immigration in 1968 – has since the early 1970s adopted "first language" and education laws to steer immigrants into the francophone community.[92] The Government of Quebec summarized the essence of its model in a 1994 policy document: "Being a Québécois means being engaged in fact in Quebec's choices for society. For the immigrant established in Quebec, adopting Quebec as an adopted land, there requires an engagement like all other citizens, and to respect these very choices of society."[93] In opposition to the Canadian *mosaic*, the preferred metaphor is that of the Quebec *tree* into which various rootstocks are grafted.[94] Nevertheless, if political rhetoric is disregarded and attention is paid to actual practices and outcomes, then Canadian multiculturalism and Quebec interculturalism have much in common. Marie Mc Andrew puts the case clearly:

> They share a high commitment to diversity, considered a major feature of collective identity, as well as a definition of equality that goes further than formal equality to include equity (both governments recognize systemic or indirect discrimination and have adopted compensatory and equalization programs). Both policies also clearly value the Human Rights perspective (whether the *Québec Charter of Human Rights and Freedoms* or the *Canadian Charter of Rights and Freedoms*) as the main framework for managing diversity.[95]

Most recently, immigration and integration issues have figured prominently on the political agenda in Quebec after the provincial government tabled its proposed Charter of Values in 2013.[96] The Charter proved to be highly controversial, and it generated considerable debate in Quebec and in the rest of Canada. Most attention was devoted to Article 5 of Chapter II: "In the exercise of their functions, personnel members of public bodies must not wear objects such as headgear, clothing, jewellery or other adornments which, by their conspicuous nature, overtly indicate a religious affiliation."[97] The Charter required state employees to remove headscarves, yarmulkes, turbans, and larger-than-average crucifixes to remain employed in the public sector. According to the Quebec government, the purpose of the bill was to establish a charter that affirms the values of state secularism, religious neutrality, and equality between women and men and provides a framework for accommodation requests. However, the Charter of Values must clearly be considered in light of the long-standing opposition to Canadian multiculturalism policy and the larger project of national affirmation.[98] Generally, Quebec voices have so far had little impact on federal immigration and integration policies, and the federal "liberal and expansionary consensus" does not seem to be overly threatened.[99] Moreover, the pre-election and election controversy over the proposed Charter appeared to contribute to the Parti Québécois's loss in the 2013 general election in Quebec.

All things considered, Canada has both presented itself and been perceived as an international model in the areas of immigration control and immigrant integration. This book presents the first systematic study of the international relevance of the Canadian model. The focus here is on the three Scandinavian countries: Denmark, Norway, and Sweden.

Policy Transfer and National Models on the International Stage

In our globalized world, countries are constantly exposed to and confronted with alternative solutions to public problems. Occasionally, the process is demand driven in the sense that domestic reformers actively search for inspiration abroad. Eleanor Westney effectively illustrates this point in her classic study of the use of apparently Western prototypes by Japan's late-nineteenth-century "modernizers" to create new governmental initiatives.[100] Apparently, the imperial government dispatched officers to study progressive judicial, military, and policing systems in France; the successful naval and postal establishments in Great Britain; and advanced banking as well as art education in the United States. In other instances, the process is supply driven; that is, national public sector reformers are more or less passive – even reluctant – receivers of externally generated reform concepts promoted by other states or international organizations. Both the neoliberal turn at the end of the 1970s and the transition from the "Old Public Administration" to the "New Public Management" in the 1990s serve as examples of dominant reform waves affecting political-administrative systems worldwide in a supply-driven way.[101]

The attention devoted to the Canadian immigration and integration policy model in Scandinavia is a product of both demand- and supply-driven mechanisms. Denmark, Norway, and Sweden have actively searched for inspiration abroad, but the Canadian model has also been promoted internationally, including in Scandinavia. This book analyses the degree of policy transfer that has occurred from Canada to Denmark, Norway, and Sweden in the area of immigration control and immigrant integration, where policy transfer is understood as a process "by which knowledge of policies, administrative arrangements, institutions, and ideas in one political setting (past or present) is used in the development of policies, administrative arrangements, institutions, and ideas in another political system."[102]

Since the 1990s, there has been a proliferation of public policy studies that directly and indirectly use, discuss, and analyse processes involved in lesson-drawing, policy convergence, policy diffusion, and policy transfer.[103] The focus here on policy transfer between countries aims to escape the "methodological nationalism" tendency of treating countries as independent units.[104] The premise is that domestic public policies are shaped not only by developments *within* nation states, but also by relationships *between* nation states. Policy transfer from other countries has, therefore, been linked to "evidence-based" policy-making, a movement in public policy governance that has received increasingly wide attention during the past decade.[105] The central idea is that countries can learn from what has been "proven" to work elsewhere.

Policy transfer, as an analytic concept, divides nations into two types: some are "borrowers" of policies from other countries and others are "lenders." While the latter categorization is often assigned to the Scandinavian countries,[106] Canada is usually described as a borrower in the public policy literature. The United States has had a particularly important influence on Canada.[107] Although much prior research has suggested that the respective roles of borrower and lender seldom change,[108] this is not a universal rule. Japan has, for instance, moved from seeking lessons from other countries to increasingly becoming an example to others.[109] This book demonstrates the ways and extent to which a traditional borrower (Canada) has acted as a model for countries often classified as lenders (the Scandinavian countries).

Policy transfer across borders is not a static process. Policy transfer can be a reciprocal exercise, that is, a process where the roles of borrower and lender change more or less continuously as countries engage in exchange processes over time. This perspective opens the potential for mutual adaptation and coevolution of public policies across borders. These reciprocal dynamics are strongly emphasized by the Canadian government in the area of immigration and integration policies:

> Canada's peaceful pluralism continues to be seen as a model of integration and social cohesion. Consequently, foreign governments and international organizations have shown an interest in Canadian multiculturalism and how our experiences can be applied to address challenges and build upon opportunities presented by their own increasingly diverse populations. The Government of Canada actively engages in discussions with other countries and other interested parties on issues of mutual concern related to immigration and increasing diversity, including racism, anti-Semitism, and other forms of discrimination. Through these discussions, the Government also learns from the challenges faced by others. CIC continues to promote Canada's experience of peaceful pluralism as a successful model.[110]

This reciprocal relationship implies a need to explore the possibility of a mutual adaptation and a search for examples in which Canada borrowed from the Scandinavian countries in the areas of immigration and integration policies.

In order to capture these dynamics, policy transfer processes must be studied over time. The study of "time" and "temporal" factors has gained increasing attention from political science and public policy/administration scholars,[111] but has often been ignored in the subfield of policy transfer studies.[112] Instead, much of the policy transfer literature has focused on questions such as "what is transferred?," "who is involved?," or "what factors constrain policy transfer processes?"[113] The lack of attention devoted to "time" and "temporality" is surprising since cross-country policy transfers gradually unfold and may take place over extended time periods. Inspired by Rich's three-stage model of knowledge utilization in organizations, subsequent chapters address this oversight by examining policy transfer as an iterative process rather than as a single, discrete event at a specific point in time.[114] The focus is on information and knowledge flow, and a central task is to investigate the regularity and duration in which information and knowledge about policies and practices travel between countries.

While policy transfers might be based on lessons drawn from the past,[115] policy-makers usually look for contemporary examples.[116] By paying attention to the regularity with which new information about policies, administrative arrangements, institutions, and ideas in another political system is gathered and processed by potential users, researchers and policy-makers are more likely to advance knowledge of the precise reasons why specific policy models rise or fall from favour. It is hypothesized that an extended time frame will allow for a deeper understanding of how policy transfers evolve.[117] In particular, a broader time frame is more suitable for capturing learning dynamics between countries characterized by long lags and complex causal chains. According to Dussauge-Laguna, "By assuming that policy transfer processes will generally take some time to unfold and show its effects, we might be in a better position to trace how foreign ideas are slowly translated, adopted and eventually absorbed by the importer jurisdiction."[118] An extended time frame is, therefore, suitable to test for policy convergence across countries, whereby policy convergence is seen as a process of "becoming" rather than a condition of "being" more alike.[119]

However, policy transfer is not an all-or-nothing process. Dolowitz and Marsh identify four different gradations of policy transfer:

- copying (direct and complete transfer of a policy or program from another jurisdiction);
- emulation (transfer of the basic ideas behind a policy or program in another jurisdiction with adjustments for different circumstances);
- combinations (transfer of policies and programs from several different jurisdictions); and
- inspiration (policy in one jurisdiction is used as an intellectual stimulus and may inspire a policy change, but the final outcomes do not actually draw upon the original).[120]

Furthermore, Evans and Davies distinguish between "hard" and "soft" policy transfer.[121] For them, hard policy transfer implies the direct transfer of specific programs and their implementation. Soft transfer, on the other hand, includes transfer of ideas, concepts, and attitudes. Based on these definitions, copying is a manifestation of hard transfer, while emulation and inspiration exemplify soft transfer. Non-transfer is also an option, if decision-makers deem foreign policies or programs to be either politically or technically undesirable or impractical in the domestic context.

It is expected that *how* the transfer occurred and *who* the key actors were in this process affect the degree of transfer. There are several ways in which policy transfer and learning from abroad can occur. For example, a reforming country may actively attempt to collect information from other countries on policy experiences through organized study trips and systematic analyses.[122] Rose refers to foreign study trips as the "gold standard" for international policy learning.[123] In other cases, reformers may be exposed to reform ideas from other countries in an informal and less organized manner.[124] Policy experts and civil servants may be associated with different degrees of policy transfer from other countries, and they may act differently from politicians. For instance, it has been assumed that politicians tend to look for "quick fix" solutions and promote copying to a greater extent than policy experts.[125] The relationships between the degrees, methods, and actors involved in policy transfer and learning processes have received little attention in the policy transfer literature.[126] The empirical discussions in this book address these relationships in three different cases, which can increase our understanding of why policy transfer occurred – if it did – and why one type of policy transfer occurred in one context and not another.

In discussing policy transfer, it is also useful to distinguish between "voluntary" and "coercive" transfer.[127] Voluntary transfer can be seen as demand driven where some form of dissatisfaction or problem with the status quo is the primary catalyst for a country to seek lessons from abroad. Both direct and indirect forms of coercive transfer are products of supply-driven mechanisms where countries are either forced to adopt a policy or to do so indirectly as a result of transnational policy externalities and mutual interdependence between states. Both voluntary and coercive forms of policy transfer between Canada and the Scandinavian countries merit consideration in the areas of immigration control and immigrant integration policies. Ultimately, this issue has to do with what role the Canadian immigration and integration policy model played in Denmark, Norway, and Sweden.

Learning from and referencing distant policy models and practices are now commonplace.[128] However, the construction and use of so-called national models in comparative migration studies have been challenged on empirical, as well as on epistemological and methodological grounds, since the early 2000s.[129] First, the idea of national models is often inspired by historical-institutionalist ideas that accentuate stability and downplay change.[130] The underlying assumption is that the conditions that led to a specific model are unlikely to change rapidly and that models themselves tend to develop a certain path-dependency or resistance to change. However, the Canadian immigration and integration policy model has changed over time. For instance, the Conservative government that came into power in 2006 adopted several changes in both policies and practices. The number of temporary foreign workers admitted to Canada increased substantially; a wide range of citizenship law amendments were implemented in order to reduce the number of "citizens of convenience" and to enhance the value of Canadian citizenship; and changes to refugee policy were introduced to crack down on so-called bogus claimants, to mention some examples. The debate on immigration and integration issues has also drifted away from the traditional liberal consensus position. For instance, the niqab, a head covering worn by some Muslim women, became a defining issue of the 2015 federal election campaign, with the Conservative Party in favour of limiting its use in certain public spaces, and the New Democratic Party (NDP) and the Liberal Party coming out strongly against such restrictions. Once the newly elected Liberal government took office, it reversed key policies on citizenship introduced by the previous government. This book embraces the view of national models as unstable and fluctuating, and seeks to identify how changes and shifts in domestic policy priorities and debates influence the international reputation of the Canadian model. Indications of an emerging convergence of policies and practices across national borders,[131] including between Canada and the Scandinavian countries, will also be subject to investigation.

Second, an intrinsic aspect and criticism of national models in comparative migration research is that they tend to be too nation-state centric.[132] Because of the focus on the "national," some claim that local variations in policies and practices may be overlooked.[133] To dodge this potential pitfall, this study has already explained the nuances between Quebec's interculturalism and Canada's multiculturalism. Also, a considerable degree of decentralization and provincial autonomy has been introduced to Canada's immigration and integration policy regime over the years in order to accommodate local needs and priorities.[134] For instance, the composition and size of immigration populations vary across the provinces, and while British Columbia grants Sikh motorcyclists a waiver from the helmet requirement, Ontario does not.[135] Despite the resulting increased complexity, federal legislation is still paramount in many areas related to immigration control and immigrant integration in Canada. The book will therefore focus on the role the Canadian immigration and integration policy model has played in the three unitary Scandinavian countries.

Third, critics claim that the use of national models, as analytic tools, tends to oversimplify policies and overemphasize the alleged coherence and consistency of policies.[136] The distinctiveness and cohesiveness of the Canadian model can clearly be challenged. Similar practices and policies can be identified elsewhere, and internal incoherencies and inconsistencies are easily observed. In terms of immigration control, Canada's open and expansive approach is comparable to that of other traditional immigrant societies like Australia, New Zealand, and the United States. In particular, the Canadian "points system," used to select high-skilled workers, was largely based on the Australian system.[137] Over the years, several other countries around the world have adopted similar selection systems. Moreover, aspects of Canada's inclusive multiculturalist approach can be found elsewhere. In fact, the Netherlands has often served as the multiculturalist policy archetype.[138] Despite similarities with other countries, the distinctiveness and defining character of the Canadian immigration and integration policy model are associated with the deeply entwined and carefully managed relationship between the policies on immigration control and immigrant integration. A former government official and now academic researcher also demarcated Canada's distinctiveness with reference to the link between its open and expansionary immigration policies and its inclusive multicultural integration policies:

> What we [Canadians] do is not unlike what the Australians do, not unlike what the New Zealanders do, and in a vague way not unlike what the Americans do. We often talk about four traditional settler countries in the world and those are the four. The thing that characterises all four is that we are open to immigration, our societies were all built on immigration, we are used to immigration, we think it works for us … Now, we are the only one among these countries with a robust model of multiculturalism. Australia's used to be like ours but it is much diminished.[139]

The cohesiveness of the Canadian model can also be questioned. In particular, policy inconsistencies with respect to the treatment of low- and high-skilled workers will be systematically addressed as these inconsistencies are assumed to have consequences for the policy transfer process and may challenge the attractiveness of the Canadian model internationally. Also, the duality and potential tension between the existence versus the perception of a distinct Canadian immigration and integration policy model may affect the Scandinavian reform debate and process. The point is that a distinct Canadian model can be powerful as a *policy frame* or *discourse*, whether it exists in practice or not. As Bertossi argues, "The model concepts are used, imagined, negotiated, affirmed, contested, and challenged by different types of people. Models should not be studied as if they exist in a stable and consistent normative, cultural, historical, and institutional context. It is critical to be aware of the diverse uses of models and the negotiations, discussions – and misunderstandings – in which they figure."[140]

Fourth, national models are not just a "matter of unilateral projection" from the models' architects towards their audience.[141] Instead, the receivers and would-be emulators of external national models play an active part in the (social) production and reproduction of these models. According to Peck and Theodore, "policy models reveal their character as 'relational' constructions; they do not simply travel, intact, from sites of invention to sites of emulation, like some superior export product, or to borrow the parlance of the field, as 'silver bullets.'"[142] As might be expected, different coalitions of actors in Scandinavia, including politicians, policy-makers, academics, experts, interest group representatives, and journalists, have contributed to the making and diffusion of what is referred to as the "Canadian immigration and integration policy model."

The Scandinavian countries have generally been described as "reluctant reformers,"[143] and in his discussion of whether there exists a distinct Scandinavian reform profile, Christensen identifies a number of similarities.[144] A main finding in his study of the New Public Management reform wave that has swept most Western countries over the past three decades is that the Scandinavian countries tend to filter, edit, and redefine external models in a "process of pragmatic adaptation."[145] To be sure, there are national variations among Denmark, Norway, and Sweden in their approach to the Canadian model as will be discussed in subsequent chapters.

Analysing the role of external models in domestic policy-making is a complex enterprise. Sometimes processes of policy transfer and learning are evident when reformers make direct references to foreign ideas and policy models. Other times, few direct references, but many indirect and less visible links between ideas and policies across countries, can be identified.[146] Both the visible and the concealed influences from Canada on the Scandinavian countries will be explored. In regard to the visible influences, countries may evoke foreign national models for different reasons. Organization theory sheds light on these reasons by distinguishing between three different theoretical perspectives: the structural-instrumental, the cultural-institutional, and the myth-based.[147]

The *structural-instrumental perspective* is based on a means-ends rationality in which policy solutions are seen as products of deliberate purpose, design, and choice among alternative arrangements. Reforms are adopted in order to realize predetermined goals and to improve policy outcomes. The Canadian immigration and integration policy model can, in this regard, be seen as an inspirational model for reforms through processes of imitation and learning. It is here expected that the references to this model by political and administrative leaders in Denmark, Norway, and Sweden will be supported by systematic analyses of the model's advantages and disadvantages in the Scandinavian context.

From a *cultural-institutional perspective*, policy solutions are seen as the outcomes of organic evolutionary processes rather than as deliberate choices at specific points in time.[148] Public policies are shaped by internal and external factors over time. References to the Canadian immigration and integration policy model, from this perspective, arise from an emerging or already existing cultural compatibility between the model and informal norms and values held in Scandinavia. A principal task is, thus, to search for shared Canadian and Scandinavian cultural traditions and historical paths that may explain the references to the Canadian immigration and integration model.

A *myth-based perspective* perceives organizational reforms in terms of myths, symbols, fashions, and trends.[149] Reforms are not considered to be about instrumental-structural design or cultural-institutional compatibility but more about the promotion of administrative reform symbols. External policy models are evoked because they are widely recognized as proper or fitting solutions by other actors in the surrounding environment. Similarly, experiences of other countries are used tactically to support or enhance the legitimacy of a decision.[150] The idea is that policy decisions are more easily defensible and look better if they are part of an international trend.[151] According to this perspective, political and administrative leaders in Scandinavia may refer to the Canadian immigration and integration policy model because it represents a symbol of success due to its glowing international reputation. It is difficult to determine whether or not an international policy solution is used solely for symbolic purposes. In some cases, public leaders may directly admit this. In others, the systematic use of value-infused concepts, slogans, and metaphors may provide clues. A discrepancy between "talk" and "action" – what Brunsson refers to as "hypocrisy" – may also be an indication of myth dynamics.[152] For instance, Scandinavian reformers may talk about and praise the Canadian immigration and integration policy model without actually undertaking practical actions.

Both the structural-instrumental and the cultural-institutional perspectives put the voluntary aspects of policy transfer at centre stage, whereas a myth-based perspective is open to coercive interpretations. However, the three perspectives are not mutually exclusive, and references to the Canadian immigration and integration policy model in Danish, Norwegian, and Swedish politics may be subject to different interpretations. Also, different actors may refer to the Canadian model for different reasons.

A structural-instrumental perspective is assumed to be important because the Scandinavian nations have been seen as highly rationalistic when it comes to policy-making.[153] Lundqvist and Petersen emphasize the alliance and interplay between science and policy in Scandinavian policy-making processes.[154] They demonstrate that scientific studies have fundamentally underpinned and paved the way for political reforms in Denmark, Norway, and Sweden throughout the twentieth century: "With the aid of social science in particular, the form and content of politics has been able to be tested and further developed. Politics has sought and gained support in academic analysis when it has wanted to expand its understanding of how society works. Academic scholars, for their part, met with a powerful ally when their chartings and theoretical investigations could be incorporated into reform efforts that were large, broad and politically anchored."[155]

Pragmatism is another essential element of Scandinavian policy-making that can be linked to a structural-instrumental perspective. A pragmatic approach implies that emphasis is placed on practical results or concerns rather than on theories or ideological principles. The historical compromises between business and labour, and the long-standing strength of social-democratic parties in Scandinavia are practical illustrations of the pragmatism between the opposing ideologies of liberal capitalism and socialism. As noted previously, Marquis Childs referred to this pragmatic solution as "The Middle Way."[156] Moreover, the emphasis on planning in the Scandinavian economic policy debate has, in part, been seen as a "practical, rational substitute for the abstract ideological discussion on state ownership versus private ownership."[157] Even the famous "Nordic Balance" between the two opposing superpowers – the

Soviet Union and the United States of America – during the Cold War can be seen as a product of the same pragmatic attitude. Also, the Scandinavian welfare state has been considered as a pragmatic solution and not the result of theoretical design: "Its dynamics change as needs and opportunities are placed on the policy agenda."[158]

Rationality and pragmatism are useful variables in evaluating the ways in which the Canadian immigration and integration policy model has been used in the Scandinavian countries during the 2000–15 period. These concepts are especially useful in assessing the interactions between experts (ranging from high-ranking, specialized civil servants to academics) and politicians in this policy domain. However, cultural-institutional dynamics are also important as the understandings of national identity and nationhood in Scandinavia gradually change and as these nations transform into diverse immigrant societies from ethnic homogeneous nation states. Through these slow-moving historical developments, the Scandinavian countries increasingly resemble traditional settler nations, like Canada. Moreover, Canada and Scandinavia already share many fundamental sociopolitical norms and values. Both inhere the traditional values associated with liberal, parliamentary democracy and boast advanced capitalist economies. Their shared commitment to the welfare state is also crucial. The links between ethnic diversity and a comprehensive welfare state, therefore, make the Canadian model increasingly relevant and appropriate as a reference point in Scandinavian debates and reform processes as Denmark, Norway, and Sweden become more ethnically diverse. These developments pinpoint Canada as an increasingly natural reference through more organic evolutionary processes rather than as a result of a rational decision at a specific point in time. Despite the similarities, there are also important differences between the Canadian and Scandinavian welfare states when it comes to immigrant integration. By contrast to the universal Scandinavian welfare states, Canada's residual welfare structure focuses on those services essential for life, and only after all other means of service provision, for instance families and charities, have been exhausted: In the case of new Canadian immigrants, much of the responsibility for embedding themselves in paid labour is expected to be self-directed with minimal assistance from service agencies.[159] Emerging trends in this direction in Scandinavian welfare policy will be identified.

Potential mutual adaptation and the coevolution of policies as a result of Canadian and Scandinavian encounters over time can also be viewed from a cultural-institutional perspective. The practice of expert exchanges and cooperation can contribute to the formation of collective identities and shared understandings among actors of what counts as "normal, truth, right and good" with respect to how specific policy issues should be dealt with.[160] Political reforms are explained and justified in value-rational terms, that is, in terms of their appropriateness not just their efficiency.[161] These exchanges can occur through bilateral contacts between Canada and individual Scandinavian countries or in a wider multilateral setting organized by international organizations.

Myth dynamics are also considered. In particular, it has been noted that the Canadian immigration and integration policy model is often portrayed as a successful (almost mythical) model by foreign public commentators and international media.[162] Politicians engaging in electoral competition may be tempted to associate themselves with such media messages without having done any systematic analyses about the Canadian model's appropriateness and suitability in a foreign context. Instead, the model can be evoked in a highly superficial manner, more like a dominant image or symbol of success. The extent to which Scandinavian media outlets and politicians have evoked the Canadian immigration and integration policy model in accordance with a myth-based perspective was possible to assess from interviews, which are described in the methodological framework of the research.

A Methodological Note

Comparative immigration policy research typically proceeds along two paths.[163] The first searches for nationally distinct approaches in managing migration flows and their political consequences, while the second seeks evidence that immigration and integration policies across countries converge as governments grapple with common problems. This book combines the two approaches, presenting evidence on how Denmark, Norway, and Sweden have been impacted by the Canadian immigration and integration policy model during the 2000–15 period.

In terms of periodization, the new millennium provides a suitable starting point for the analysis since it has generally been considered to represent the beginning of a "reassessment phase" in the history of Scandinavian immigration and integration policies.[164] Similarly, 2015 seems like a natural cut-off date due to the extraordinary political developments, like the introduction of temporary border checks and passport requirements, that were triggered by the refugee crisis that engulfed Europe in the second half of 2015, when Scandinavia received annual record numbers of asylum seekers within a few months. In total for 2015, Denmark, Norway, and Sweden respectively received 20,935, 31,145, and 162,450 asylum seekers from a number of countries, but mainly from Syria.[165] Likewise, the Canadian context changed significantly with the new Liberal government taking office in November 2015. The new government not only reversed a number of restrictive policies related to citizenship, but also opened up for a more "compassionate" approach to refugees in light of the ongoing crisis. References will be made to the dynamic developments in both Canada and Scandinavia in 2015 in the subsequent chapters, although the precise long-term policy consequences are still uncertain.

Domestic public policies are shaped both by developments *within* nation states and by relationships *between* nation states. Therefore both the wider external and the narrower national context of Scandinavian immigration and integration policies must be addressed. To be sure, immigration and integration polices in Denmark, Norway, and Sweden have become increasingly internationalized over the past decades. For instance, Scandinavian policies are subject to European Union (EU) policy-making and legislation in several areas. This is true for Denmark and Sweden as full members, but also for Norway, which is effectively attached to the EU through a number of comprehensive agreements, such as the European Economic Area (EEA) Agreement and the Schengen cooperation. Free movement of persons, which entitles every EU citizen to live in any EU/EEA country, is a fundamental right guaranteed by the EU to its citizens. The Schengen cooperation enhances this freedom by enabling citizens to cross internal borders without being subjected to border checks. Although it remains a key objective to develop a uniform and comprehensive European migration policy, the member states still retain the right to determine admission rates for people coming from third countries to seek work, for instance. Also, while the EU may promote incentives and support for measures taken by the member states to promote the integration of legally admitted third-country nationals, there is currently no provision for the harmonization of national laws and regulations. Member states also have the last words in most areas pertaining to the welfare state. Accordingly, Denmark, Norway, and Sweden still enjoy much sovereignty when it comes to developing their own immigration and integration policies. The EU dimension will in this book be addressed only when it directly impacts the role of the Canadian model in the three Scandinavian countries.

Although this study focuses on the influence of the Canadian model, Scandinavian countries have devoted attention to immigration and integration policy solutions in a number of different nations. Often the basic instincts of Denmark, Norway, and Sweden – due to their geographical proximity as well as to shared historical, cultural, economic, social, and political features – are to look first at each other. Many political and administrative solutions have resulted from mutual learning processes *internally* among the Scandinavian countries. Indeed, it has been argued that "Norway simply imported integration ideology from Sweden" in the early 1970s.[166] Norway's intensive focus on Swedish practices and policies lasted until the 1990s but then increasingly shifted to the Danish approach.[167] However, immigration and integration policies in other countries in Europe and elsewhere have also received attention in this Scandinavian reassessment phase. The Dutch integration model has, for instance, been influential across Europe. Although the "combinations" option of policy transfer is a useful category, for analytic purposes the focus in this book will be on estimating qualitatively the degree of transfer from the Canadian immigration and integration policy model to the Scandinavian countries. References to other "national models" will be made if they can shed light on this issue. The argument is not, however, that the Canadian immigration and integration policy model is the *only* influence on Scandinavia.

Policy transfer in the forms of copying and emulation may be relatively easy to detect and measure since a direct relationship can be drawn between policies, administrative arrangements, institutions, and ideas in two political systems. However, inspiration is also a powerful form of policy transfer that can lead to significant changes, although the links between policy lenders and borrowers are less obvious. Inspiration can be seen as a type of soft transfer that inspires fresh thinking about a policy problem and in this way helps to facilitate policy change.[168] Since inspirational models can engender different changes in different countries, tracing and following the Canadian immigration and integration model in the Scandinavian context require an explorative approach. While policy-making tends to be an intricate and often a partially hidden process, Scandinavian policy-making appears to be relatively open and transparent because policy reform processes involve extensive consultation and information gathering. Researchers therefore have access to a wealth of governmental and parliamentary reports as well as to a wide variety of key actors involved in the policy-making processes. Accordingly, the empirical basis for this book comprises an extensive review of existing studies of immigration and integration policy reform processes, systematic analyses of public documents including proposals submitted by government to parliaments, documents from parliamentary debates, reports by ad hoc expert commissions, and letters from consulted agencies. Media debates from the three countries were also collected and analysed. In addition, thirty-two semi-structured interviews were conducted with key politicians, high-ranking civil servants, and policy experts involved in immigration and integration policy in the three Scandinavian countries and in Canada. Both the collected documents and the transcribed interviews were analysed in relation to the theoretical framework presented above.

Dynamic, interactive, in-depth interviews have a great potential for exposing the wider and deeper context of political processes. However, there are obvious limitations to interviews and conversations with powerful policy actors, who often "yield exaggerated accounts of foresight, rationality, worldly connectivity, or creative entrepreneurism."[169] Hence, interviews were conducted and interpreted from a critical distance. Most importantly, in order to promote candid and forthright responses, interviewees were assured that they would not be identified and that their responses to questions would remain confidential. Further, responses were cross-checked, and interview data were corroborated with information obtained from written sources. Although the interviews were largely unstructured and tailored to the position and experience of the respective respondents, a few common questions were put to all. Above all, each interviewee (whether Canadian or Scandinavian) was asked to express his or her personal understanding of the defining characteristic of the Canadian immigration and integration policy model and its role as an international model. The interviews were particularly geared towards exposing a potential distinction between the existence versus the perception of a distinct Canadian immigration and integration policy model in the Scandinavian reform debate and process.

Collectively, the sources were aimed at uncovering both the nature of the Canadian model and the outcomes of the policy transfer process. A number of key questions guided the project and the analysis:

• To what extent does a distinct Canadian immigration and integration policy model exist (perceived or real)?

- What are the main policy components of the Canadian model (real or perceived)?
- Why is the Canadian model attractive for would-be reformers internationally?
- What was the overall impact of the Canadian model on the recent reform process in Denmark, Norway, and Sweden?
- Through which processes did Scandinavian institutions and actors approach the Canadian model?
- Was the learning from Canada coordinated or fragmented in terms of actors and organizations?
- To what extent were central political leaders involved in this policy transfer and learning process compared to administrative leaders and policy experts?
- What were the main challenges in this learning process?
- Did the Scandinavian reformers take a broad and comprehensive perspective, trying to adopt the Canadian immigration and integration policy model as a complete package of administrative reforms, or did they pick out only certain elements for attention?
- Were efforts made to learn not only from alleged successes but also from the problems and negative experiences from Canada?
- Did the Canadian model play different roles in the three Scandinavian countries?
- Did Canada learn lessons about immigration and integration from the Scandinavian countries?

Although Sweden experienced its first waves of immigration earlier than Denmark and Norway, the experiences and challenges facing the Scandinavian countries in this area of public policy are similar. During the 2000–15 period, both the policies governing the control of the influx of immigrants and those governing how immigrants are treated once they have entered the country were reassessed in all three countries. This book provides a systematic and theoretically oriented analysis of both similarities and differences in the role the Canadian immigration and integration policy model has played in the recent and ongoing reform process in Denmark, Norway, and Sweden.

The Plan of the Book

A systematic study of Canada's international leadership role in immigration and integration policy in the Scandinavian context between 2000 and 2015 can produce practical insights – with the potential for improving public policy outcomes – in both Scandinavia and Canada. First, immigration and integration policy has been linked to the long-term survival of the comprehensive welfare state systems in Scandinavia. The Canadian model is particularly relevant for Denmark, Norway, and Sweden because Canada has successfully combined an open and accommodating approach to immigration and increasing ethnic diversity with a comprehensive welfare state system.

Second, the book addresses one of the main goals of Canada's foreign policy, which is to promote a greater understanding and appreciation internationally of Canada and "Canadian values." According to the Canadian government, one of three central objectives of the Multiculturalism Program is to "actively engage in discussions on multiculturalism at the international level."[170] Subsequent chapters will assess the extent to which this goal has been reached.

General theoretical insights on policy transfer and learning processes across countries will also be drawn from this Canadian-Scandinavian case study on immigration and integration policy. In particular, a gap in the current literature will be filled by increasing our understanding of how policy transfer processes and outcomes are shaped by the institutional settings and governance regimes in which they take place. The relationship between the actual *degree* of policy transfer observed, the *actors* involved, and the *methods* used in these processes will be assessed. The possibility of policy transfer and learning processes as potentially reciprocal exercises will also be explored and evaluated.

To achieve these aims, the book is organized as follows: chapters 2, 3, and 4 in part II assess the role of the Canadian immigration and integration policy model in Denmark, Norway, and Sweden between 2000 and 2015. Due to its status as a pioneering country in terms of Scandinavian immigration and integration policy, Sweden will be covered first, followed by Denmark and Norway.

Part III includes two chapters. Chapter 5 connects policy transfer and lesson-drawing from Canada with the domestic policy-making style in Scandinavia, while chapter 6 presents the main conclusions and a discussion of the future of the Canadian model.

To be sure, the Canadian immigration and integration policy model is an internationally recognized model that has shaped the reform debates and processes in all three Scandinavian countries during the past decade. The book therefore demonstrates that the Canadian model, often perceived as a product of unique and favourable domestic circumstances, can still be relevant in other countries. However, dark clouds on the horizon for the Canadian model are also identified. The increased reliance on foreign temporary workers and a declining proportion of refugees in relation to economic immigrants may over time challenge the Canadian model's international reputation.

The Canadian Immigration and Integration Policy Model in Scandinavian Politics

Sweden's Special Transatlantic Policy Relationship: Moving towards Mutual Inspiration

We have an international obligation to receive refugees and we need foreign labour, but we would also like that the immigrants stay, build a home, feel at home and become citizens – it is to achieve this we look to Canada.

High-ranking Swedish civil servant[1]

Sweden is currently portrayed as an exception to the common European trend towards a "retreat from multiculturalism."[2] Instead, Sweden's approach has emerged as a European model of multicultural policy much like the Canadian model in North America. In fact, a special relationship has evolved between Canada and Sweden in the area of immigration and integration policy since the early 2000s, despite differences in certain policy priorities and practices. Their close transatlantic policy relationship has been clearly articulated by Canadian and Swedish politicians and senior civil servants. Moreover, the relationship is increasingly reciprocal, showing signs of mutual inspiration, adaptation, and coevolution of policies between the two countries.

This chapter demonstrates empirically the role that the Canadian immigration and integration policy model has played in the Swedish reform process in the 2000–15 period. A second aim is to illustrate how the relationship over time has become increasingly reciprocal with Canadians also devoting increasing attention towards Swedish policies and practices in the areas of immigration control and immigrant integration. The bilateral exchanges between politicians, public servants, representatives of non-governmental organizations, and academics in the two countries have also increasingly fostered the formation of emerging collective identities and shared understandings among Canadian and Swedish actors within the field.

Reforming Swedish Immigration and Integration Policies

Sweden's immigration and integration policies have traditionally been marked by low degrees of politicized contestation by contrast to its Scandinavian counterparts. Anti-immigration parties enjoyed little success until the Sweden Democrats obtained 5.7 per cent of the votes and gained representation in Parliament after the 2010 general election, a success that was even surpassed in the subsequent election. Nevertheless, immigration control and immigrant integration have received substantial political attention in Sweden since the early 2000s. The Swedish reform process reflects both comprehensive transformations and gradual adaptations of established principles and practices.

The long dormant issue of labour immigration rose to the top of the political agenda during the 2002 election campaign when centre-right parties argued in favour of opening the country to labour immigration from countries outside the European Union (EU). The bill that was finally adopted in 2008 represented a clear liberalization of existing policies.[3] According to the new legislation, a temporary work permit could be granted to foreigners who had a job offer to sustain self-support. In addition, a person who has held a residence permit during the past five years because of employment for a total of four years could then be granted a permanent resident permit. Moreover, an asylum seeker with a rejected application could apply for a residency permit as a labour immigrant on the condition that the person had already been employed for at least six months and could show that the job would last for an additional year. Although the Swedish government actively promoted the new demand-driven labour migration policy of openness, flexibility, and efficiency as a role model for other countries to follow, the 2008 reform did not produce a dramatic increase in the number of work permits granted in Sweden.[4] According to the Swedish Migration Agency, the number of work permits increased from approximately 14,500 in 2008 to 17,000 in 2015. This means that labour immigration to Sweden still only accounts for a small portion of total immigration to the country and is dwarfed by the numbers for both refugees and family reunifications.

Sweden's long-standing international reputation as a country with a generous and humanitarian refugee policy was reconfirmed during this period.[5] For example, large numbers of Iraqi refugees, ineligible for asylum according to the Geneva Convention, were recognized as people "in need of protection" by Swedish authorities. In fact, Sweden has welcomed more refugees from Iraq than has any other EU country. Sweden's generous humanitarian refugee policy was further demonstrated in 2013 when Sweden announced that it would be the first EU member state to grant permanent residency to all Syrian refugees seeking asylum who had already fled to the country.

Openness is also apparent in Swedish policies for family reunification, in that sponsors are not required to financially support relatives moving to the country. As a result, family immigrants have comprised by far the largest group of immigrants to Sweden in recent decades.[6] However, in 2010 the centre-right government, in the face of substantial criticism from the opposition, introduced a modest financial support requirement.[7] According to the new rules, a person living in Sweden must be able to document a regular income sufficient for self-support and prove the availability of adequate accommodation for both sponsor and immigrant. Thus, the rule does not require sponsors in Sweden to financially support their relatives, but only to be able to support themselves. The new regulation was introduced to promote immigrant integration so that persons who are successful in finding jobs and residences can be "'rewarded' by being allowed to have their family come to Sweden."[8]

Further, Sweden is often described as a prominent representative of an officially declared multiculturalism policy.[9] Despite the alleged retreat from multiculturalism in several European countries during the 2000s,[10] the Swedish Parliament's adoption of an official multicultural policy in 1975 can still be recognized in the country's approach to immigrant integration.[11] For instance, the comparatively short time required for residents to obtain citizenship – five years – has remained unchanged since 1975. Despite an increased emphasis on individual immigrants' obligations over the past decade, Sweden has rejected the introduction of formal language requirements and tests of knowledge as conditions for naturalization. The decision to allow dual citizenship (or even multiple citizenship) from 2001 is consistent with a multicultural approach to immigrant integration, in which citizenship is regarded as a tool of integration and not a reward for successful integration.[12] Barriers to citizenship were lowered again in 2014, when Parliament decided to improve opportunities for children and young people in obtaining Swedish citizenship.[13] Among other changes, the new rules state that children will acquire Swedish citizenship at birth if one of the child's parents is a Swedish citizen. In addition, the time period for obtaining citizenship was reduced for children of parents without Swedish citizenship. All in all, Swedish naturalization policies have been found to be among the least "ethnic" (as opposed to "civic") among twenty-six Western immigrant-receiving democracies.[14]

According to the international Multiculturalism Policy Index, Swedish multiculturalism policies were significantly strengthened between 2000 and 2010, with an increase from 5 to 7 out of 8 points on the index.[15] One important reason for this gain is that Sweden has become increasingly open-minded about accepting religious garments (turbans, headscarves, and skullcaps) in official workplaces where uniforms are used. These rights were confirmed in the Discrimination Act, passed in 2008.[16] The act explicitly states that employers are responsible for ensuring that "the working conditions are suitable for all employees regardless of sex, ethnicity, religion or other belief."[17] The lack of "affirmative action for disadvantaged immigrant groups" prevented Sweden from attaining a perfect score on the index. A proposal to provide affirmative action for disadvantaged immigrant groups was rejected in Sweden in 2008 to avoid stigmatizing these groups.[18]

It has been argued that the Swedish approach to immigrant integration, based on voluntary and pluralistic principles, largely resembles the Canadian model.[19] This is perhaps not surprising because the Canadian approach to multiculturalism supposedly provided transnational inspiration for the development of the Swedish policy of multiculturalism during the 1970s.[20] In fact, in an article published in 1971, Stein Rokkan advised Sweden to give up its assimilationist position in favour of the "kanadensiska alternativet," understood as "active multiculturalism."[21] Mats Wickström claims that Rokkan's article is a good example of how Canada, almost immediately upon adopting multiculturalism as an official policy in 1971, became a reference for advocates of multiculturalism in Sweden.[22] However, Canada's inspiration has endured.

"Kanadamodellen" in the Swedish Reform Debate and Process

Other Scandinavian and European countries continue to be important reference points in the Swedish debate, but the Canadian immigration and integration policy model has received extensive and persistent attention in Sweden during the recent reassessment phase. Politicians and media outlets – from left to right – have consistently referred to Canada as a potential model for Sweden. In fact, Swedish migration researcher Henrik Emilsson claims that "no country has been used more as an example of a successful immigration and integration policy" than

Canada in Sweden during the 2000s.[23] Many Canadian policy measures have been cited in the debate on reforms, but the overriding – and somewhat abstract – theme in the debate has been that immigrants could be a positive resource for Sweden just like they appear to be in Canada.

FORES, an influential Swedish think tank that invited a group of Canadian and Swedish researchers and academics to present the Canadian model to a Swedish audience in the publication *Kanadamodellen*, provided a more systematic contribution to the public debate.[24] The dominant question posed in that book is, "Vad kan Sverige lära av Kanadas modell för invandring och integration?" (What can Sweden learn from the Canadian model of immigration and integration?). In response, three essential elements of Canada's approach are emphasized: positive attitudes towards immigrants; the prominence of civil society in integration efforts; and the importance of integrating immigrants into the labour market. The future of the Swedish welfare state is an underlying concern, and although the editors assert that it would be unrealistic to copy the Canadian model, they claim that it "points at large underutilized possibilities."[25] The Swedish minister of integration, Erik Ullenhag, participated in the official launch of *Kanadamodellen*, which took place at the Embassy of Canada to Sweden in March 2011. The book generated considerable attention in the Swedish political debate.

Think tanks, particularly the green and liberal think tank, FORES, have played a key role promoting knowledge about the Canadian model to Swedish audiences. However, foreign interested parties provide selective images of the Canadian model. The relative distinctiveness of the model is sometimes exaggerated, and historical fluctuations and internal incoherencies or challenges are often undercommunicated or neglected. As emphasized by Peck and Theodore, national policy models do not simply travel intact but reveal their character as "relational" constructions.[26] In this sense, Swedish think tanks (often in tandem with Canadian stakeholders) contribute to the (social) production and reproduction of the Canadian model in the Swedish context. The crux of FORES's construction of the Canadian immigration and integration policy model is that it quickly transforms immigrants to contributing workers.

FORES's attraction to the Canadian model continues, and as a background for their future work on immigrant integration, two representatives travelled to Ottawa and Toronto on a study tour in early March 2016. The excursion was partially financed by the Embassy of Canada to Sweden,[27] another indication that the promotion of the Canadian model in Sweden often is a collaborative project among Canadian and Swedish actors.

Swedish politicians and public servants at senior levels have also paid close attention to the Canadian immigration and integration policy model for a long time. Government-created ad hoc inquiry commissions and committees, whose conclusions and recommendations are published in the government's official report series, have been principal participants in this process. The Family Immigration Committee (Anhörigkommittén), which argued for the introduction of a financial support requirement in its final report in 2002, makes numerous references to Canada.[28] In a chapter addressing international rules for family integration, Canada and the United States received special attention in addition to a group of European countries. As a background for its deliberations, the committee relied on information provided by the immigration authorities in these countries. The committee's secretariat also visited the Embassy of Canada to Sweden to learn more about the Canadian family integration system, the only country receiving this form of attention.[29]

Systematic attention to the Canadian model can also be identified in the debate on labour immigration, where Canada is recognized as a "role model," an "international pioneer," and a "world leading nation."[30] The Labour Immigration Committee (Kommittén för arbetskraftsinvandring), which began its work in 2004, refers extensively to Canada in its 2005 and 2006 reports.[31] The 2005 report, which provides an overview of the international context, contains several specific endorsements of Canadian immigration policies, and remarks that "in Canada, the view on immigration is fundamentally positive. It is generally accepted that immigration is necessary to ensure continued economic development."[32] Significantly, the committee also contends that there is a positive relationship between labour immigration and refugees in Canada: "Labour immigration makes asylum seekers more accepted, among the general public and among employers."[33]

Despite the special consideration granted to the Canadian model in the area of labour immigration, Swedish policies differ significantly from Canadian policies and practices. In general, Sweden is less selective with regard to admissions. While Canada's "points system" explicitly gives priority to high-skilled over low-skilled labour, the Swedish approach focuses on employer demands for labour, for high-skilled as well as low-skilled workers. The deeply entwined relationship between immigration control and immigrant integration has earlier been identified as the main defining feature of the Canadian model. The fact that Canada's selective and carefully managed immigration strategy contributes to maximize integration and minimize immigrants' reliance on state support and the welfare budgets is here important. However, despite the potential benefits of a more selective strategy, an immigration and integration policy expert at a Swedish think tank pointed to an ideological and cultural incompatibility between the Canadian-style points system and central Swedish values related to the equal worth of all people: "To put points on human beings is a very distant idea in Sweden."[34] Yet, an official at the Canadian embassy in Sweden was perplexed by the Swedish reservations about the points system: "I think it is an extremely strange way of looking at things because you give people marks at school, and if you are an employer and you have one opening and fifty applicants, you select the one person you want."[35] His puzzlement was widely shared among both Canadian and Danish interviewees. One may speculate that Sweden resists points-based selection systems because immigrants – high-skilled economic immigrants included – are viewed as a vulnerable group that must be protected against competitive forces and pressures. In Canada, on the other hand, economic immigrants are considered to be a strong asset and necessary to build and grow the domestic economy.

Several high-ranking public servants claimed that the private sponsorship of refugees in Canada also represents a clear misfit with Swedish welfare state ideology, based on values like universalism and equality.[36] In Sweden, ensuring that all refugees will have exactly the same services seems to be priority number one. At the same time, interviewees indicated that Sweden is interested in the way Canada has managed to engage civil society and NGOs to complement the work of local and central authorities.[37]

A former Canadian government official with extensive international experience in the immigration and integration policy field articulates the difference between Canada and Sweden:

> Every time I have spoken in Sweden, people in the audience have accused me as a Canadian or accused Canada of abusing vulnerable human beings: that we cherry-pick our migrants – even refugees – and when they arrive here, the government does not look after them but leaves them to civil society organizations to look after them, and many of those civil society organizations are run by immigrants. You leave immigrants to themselves.

> Whereas in Sweden, we look after them – hold them in our arms and rock them back and forth and pet them: a totally different approach. My only response is that yes, this is how we do it in Canada because we think it is better for the immigrants … We like to think that through the NGO sector, we empower migrants to become participating citizens of our country. Whereas we would argue that in Sweden you disempower them by doing everything for them.[38]

In terms of immigrant integration, the Swedish government appointed a parliamentary committee to consider the need to amend citizenship legislation. The Citizenship Committee (1997 års medborgarskapskommitté) delivered its first report in 1997 and a final report with detailed recommendations in 1999.[39] As a background for its deliberations, the committee devoted substantial attention to integration policies in various countries. Although much of its thinking was devoted to the Nordic countries and to a group of other European countries, Canada was also included as a case representing the wider international community. The Canadian case was fully examined during the deliberations on dual citizenship and on related language requirements for citizenship. Ultimately, a majority on the committee recommended changing the existing law, dating back to the 1950s, to accept dual citizenship. However, the committee was opposed to the introduction of language requirements for citizenship, thus departing from Canadian practices. Nevertheless, the Citizenship Inquiry (Medborgarskapsutredningen) proposed in 2013 a "language bonus" giving those who have command of the Swedish language an opportunity to obtain citizenship one year earlier than otherwise stipulated.[40]

Overall, the major emphasis in Sweden, contrary to Canada, has been to provide incentives rather than obligations for immigrant integration. This orientation is evident in the organization of citizenship ceremonies. Participation is voluntary, and there is no requirement to take an oath of allegiance. By comparison, in Canada, new citizens are legally required to attend a citizenship ceremony and to take the Oath of Citizenship. However, the creation of a citizenship ceremony in Sweden was inspired by Canadian practices.[41] The fact that numerous Swedish politicians have attended Canadian citizenship ceremonies during the last decade supports this impression. As late as March 2013, for instance, the minister of integration and several representatives from the Ministry of Employment attended a citizenship ceremony in Toronto.

Although Swedish policy-makers favour and concentrate on different aspects of the complex empirical reality referred to as the "Canadian model," their references are generally supported by systematic studies analysing its advantages and disadvantages in the Swedish context. Official study trips to Canada have contributed significantly to the knowledge base. An official at the Embassy of Sweden in Ottawa estimated that almost a hundred members of the Swedish Parliament visited Canada during a three-year period in order to learn more about the Canadian immigration and integration policy model.[42] The increased popularity of Canada as a destination for Swedish parliamentary committees is clearly evident in a study produced by the Swedish Parliamentary Evaluation and Research Unit.[43] While there were twelve study trips to Canada during the 1971–87 period, the number increased to nineteen during the 1997–2013 period. The number of study trips to the US increased from twenty-two to twenty-six during the same interval. All in all, Canada was the fifth most popular study-trip destination for Swedish parliamentary committees during the 1997–2013 period, after the EU "capital" Brussels in Belgium (sixty-three), the US (twenty-six), Finland (twenty-three), and Norway (twenty-two).

A key official at Citizenship and Immigration Canada (CIC) confirms that there has been an overwhelming Swedish interest in the Canadian model: "We have had quite a number of incoming delegations from Scandinavian governments, primarily from Sweden. They seem to be endlessly interested in what they, I think rather simplistically, call the 'Canadian model' … We have been surprised by the number and the scope of the visits."[44] Although this official questions whether a distinct Canadian immigration and integration policy exists, he recognizes that the perception of such a model is strong among Swedish visitors.

The Embassy of Canada to Sweden is often contacted by Swedish delegations prior to their study trips. According to a long-serving official at the embassy, the interest in Canada intensified significantly after the Swedish Labour Immigration Committee was established in 2004. Since then, the embassy has no longer needed to actively promote the Canadian model because the embassy is "usually approached directly by the Swedes."[45] Also, the Embassy of Sweden in Ottawa assists the various travelling delegations to establish a study-tour program while in Canada. The programs are quite comprehensive, including meetings with a wide spectrum of representatives from Canadian groups and institutions. Due to the public accessibility of official documents in Sweden, it is possible to provide specific examples of such study trips.

For instance, between 27 October and 3 November 2012, the Committee on Social Insurance of the Swedish Parliament (Riksdagens socialutskott) visited Canada to learn more about the Canadian immigration and integration model. The delegation consisted of eighteen members of Parliament along with four staff members. During five working days in Ottawa and Toronto, the committee had formal meetings with a large number of Canadian groups and institutions in the areas of immigration control and immigrant integration, including the following:

- Citizenship and Immigration Canada
- Human Resources and Skills Development Canada
- Immigration and Refugee Board of Canada
- Somali Centre for Family Services in Ottawa
- Ontario Ministry of Citizenship and Immigration
- Legislative Assembly of Ontario
- Ontario Ministry of Finance
- Ralph Chiodo Family Immigrant Reception Centre

One year after this study trip, between 29 August and 5 September 2013, Swedish members of Parliament from the Conservative Moderate Party visited many of the same institutions in Ottawa and Toronto. According to a representative at the Embassy of Sweden in Ottawa, Citizenship and Immigration Canada (CIC) is a very popular destination for Swedish visitors. Due to the repeated requests for meetings with the same institutions, the Swedish embassy is often required to explain that "it is another parliamentary delegation from the one that visited you last month" that is now interested.[46] However, Canadian officials and institutions are generally very open and welcoming towards requests for visits, at least according to a well-placed senior official at the CIC.[47] This openness is perhaps not surprising given that engaging in international discussions on multiculturalism is a central objective of Canada's Multiculturalism Program.[48]

In the aftermath of study trips, summary reports are usually written and made available to interested parties. The report on a study trip by a parliamentary delegation to Canada between 31 January and 4 February 2011 serves as an example.[49] In addition to the names of participants, the report contains information about the background and objectives of the trip plus detailed summaries of various meetings. The explicit objective of this particular trip was to "study the Canadian practices with respect to political questions related to immigration, integration and aboriginal peoples."[50] The Swedish delegation met with both the Speakers of the Senate and the House of Commons, Nôel Kinsella and Peter Milliken, respectively. In these conversations, the active and productive Swedish-Canadian parliamentary relationship was praised.

Meetings of representatives of the political executives from both countries have also occurred in the areas of immigration control and immigrant integration. Responsible ministers in the Canadian and Swedish governments have met formally several times in bilateral exchanges during the past few years. The Canadian minister of citizenship, immigration and multiculturalism, Jason Kenney, visited various institutions in Sweden in October 2012. In one significant event, Kenney participated with then Swedish minister for migration and asylum policy, Tobias Billström, among others, in a seminar hosted by the FORES think tank, which had published *Kanadamodellen* the previous year.[51] During their meeting, Kenney and Billström focused their discussions on labour immigration reforms. Kenney summarizes the impression from his trip to Stockholm in the following manner: "[I] found enormous interest in the Canadian approach. I had the impression that Sweden was trying to emulate aspects of the Canadian human capital model, but was frustrated that immigration had overwhelmingly been characterized by refugee resettlement."[52] Also during the visit to Sweden, Kenney named the main function room of the Embassy of Canada in Stockholm as the Raoul Wallenberg Room after the Swedish World War II hero who rescued tens of thousands of Jews in Hungary.[53] Apart from the important official Canadian-Swedish relationship in these matters, Billström emphasized the personal relationship between himself and Kenney during his time as minister for migration and asylum policy in the Swedish government between 2006 and 2014.[54]

In the aftermath of Kenney's trip to Sweden, the Swedish minister for integration, Erik Ullenhag, spent three days on a formal visit to Canada in March 2013 where he met and discussed immigrant integration issues with certain deputy ministers, members of Parliament, representatives from various NGOs, academics, police officers, and journalists. In the report from this trip, the Swedish minister's participation in a citizenship ceremony is accentuated.[55]

Members of other governmental institutions in Sweden have also conducted study trips to Canada. In October 2002, members of the Swedish Migration Board (Migrationsverket) visited Canada. In June 2004, representatives from the Swedish Integration Board visited Ottawa and Toronto where they met with a large number of civil servants representing different sectors and levels of government, NGO representatives, and policy practitioners as well as academics and experts on immigration and integration policy. Table 2 provides a list of just some of the Swedish delegations that have visited Canada since 2000.

Table 2 reveals that the frequency and scale of visits continued after the new centre-left government replaced the centre-right government, subsequent to the Swedish general election of September 2013. In fact, 2015 was exceptionally busy in terms of Swedish study trips to Canada. An official from the Embassy of Sweden in Ottawa claimed that it was necessary for the "new" centre-left ministers with immigration and integration portfolios to visit Canada as early as possible.[56] The frequency and scale of visits to Canada also indicate that Swedish stakeholders are sensitive to fluctuations and changes in the Canadian immigration and integration policy model over time.

In addition to the bilateral meetings between Canadian and Swedish politicians and civil servants, exchanges on immigration and integration policy issues occur in a wide variety of multilateral settings.[57] Swedish bureaucrats underscore two international forums as being particularly important in regard to Canadian-Swedish exchanges.[58] First, Canada and Sweden are two among sixteen participating states in the Intergovernmental Consultations on Migration, Asylum and Refugees (IGC).[59] Sweden acted as chair of the IGC in 2007–08.

Second, the Transatlantic Council on Migration is a deliberative body that was launched in 2008 to address policy issues and to inform migration policy-making processes across the Atlantic community in North America and Europe. The council is an initiative of the Migration Policy Institute, which is an independent, non-partisan and non-profit think tank in Washington, DC, dedicated to analysis of the movement of people worldwide. Sweden is an active participant and is one among five governments providing financial support for the council, which convenes twice a year and also holds extraordinary meetings as necessary. Sweden decided to participate in the Transatlantic Council on Migration in order to "generate more knowledge, particularly from Canada and the US."[60]

The notion of a Canadian inspirational immigration and integration policy model in which immigrants represent a positive resource clearly exists in Sweden, even though the Canadian model is not perceived or treated as institutionally consistent, normatively coherent, and historically stable. The perception that the Canadian model is distinct and successful has led to systematic attention to the model's various

Table 2. Visits to Canada from Swedish groups and institutions studying the Canadian immigration and integration policy model (2000–15)*

Swedish group/institution in Canada	Participants	Groups/institutions visited in Canada**
Committee on Labour Market of the Swedish Parliament, Ottawa, 29 February–2 March 2000	10	Human Resources and Skills Development Canada (HRSDC); World Skills Employment Services (NGO working on enhancing the economic integration of immigrants, refugees, and newcomers). Attended job application workshop for immigrants
Committee on Social Insurance of the Swedish Parliament, Victoria, 29 August 2000	8	Ministry of Multiculturalism and Immigration, British Columbia
Swedish Migration Board, Ottawa, 2 October 2002	2	Citizenship and Immigration Canada (CIC)
Committee on Social Insurance of the Swedish Parliament, Toronto/ Ottawa/Montreal, 19–24 January 2004	18	CIC; Immigration Refugee Board (IRB); Ministère des Relations avec les Citoyens et l'Immigration, Government of Quebec. Attended citizenship ceremony in Montreal
Delegation from the government's "Study of power, integration and structural discrimination," Toronto, 14–15 May 2004	3	Urban Alliance on Race Relations, Toronto; Canadian Race Relations Foundation, Toronto
Swedish Integration Board, Ottawa and Toronto, 14–19 June 2004	3	CIC; HRSDC; Department of Canadian Heritage; Ministry of Citizenship and Immigration, Government of Ontario; Skills for Change (NGO), Toronto; Afghan Women's Counselling and Integration Community Support Organization. Attended citizenship ceremony in Toronto
Swedish Association of Local Authorities and Regions (SALAR), Toronto, February 2005	19	Not available
SALAR, British Columbia,12–16 February 2006	18	Not available
Delegation of members of the Swedish Parliament, Ottawa/Toronto, 31 January–4 February, 2011	5	CIC; Standing Committee on Aboriginal Affairs and Northern Development and Standing Committee on Citizenship and Immigration in the Canadian Parliament; Assembly of First Nations; Ministry of Citizenship and Immigration, Government of Ontario; Somali Youth Association of Toronto
Committee on Social Insurance of the Swedish Parliament, Ottawa/Toronto, 27 October–3 November 2012	22	CIC; HRSDC; IRB; Somali Centre for Family Services; Ministry of Citizenship and Immigration, Government of Ontario; Ralph Chiodo Family Immigrant Reception Centre; Parliament of Canada; Legislative Assembly of Ontario

(Continued)

Table 2. Visits to Canada from Swedish groups and institutions studying the Canadian immigration and integration policy model (2000–15)*
(Continued)

Swedish group/institution in Canada	Participants	Groups/institutions visited in Canada**
Delegation of members of the Swedish Parliament, Toronto, 14–16 January 2013	2	Ministry of Citizenship and Immigration, Government of Ontario; Maytree Foundation; Toronto Region Immigrant Employment Council
Delegation led by the Swedish Minister of Integration, Ottawa, 19–21 March 2013	4	CIC; Centre for International Migration and Settlement Studies, Carleton University. Attended citizenship ceremony in Toronto
Delegation of members of the Swedish Parliament representing the Conservative Moderate Party, Ottawa, 29 August– 5 September 2013	4	CIC; HRSDC
Delegation of members of the Sweden-Canada Parliamentary Association, Ottawa/Toronto, 7–11 October 2013	5	Maytree Foundation; Toronto Region Immigrant Employment Council; Metropolis
Delegation of members of the Swedish Parliament, Toronto, 24–27 February 2015	5	Meetings with Ministry of Citizenship, Immigration and International Trade, Government of Ontario; Ryerson Maytree Global Diversity Exchange; Ralph Chiodo Family Immigrant Reception Centre
Delegation led by the Swedish Minister for Upper Secondary School and Adult Education and Training, Edmonton, 26–27 March 2015	10	Meetings with education officials concerning the integration of immigrants into the school system
Delegation led by Swedish Minister of Labour, Ottawa/Winnipeg, 9–12 June 2015	Not available	Meeting with Canadian Minister of Citizenship and Immigration; CIC; Ottawa Community Immigrant Services Organization

* Based on information obtained through Embassy of Sweden in Ottawa. (The list includes only visits that were organized by the embassy.)
** Not a complete program of visits. Only a selection of the groups and institutions visited are presented in this table.

components. This has, in turn, shaped both the reform debate and the policy-making process in Sweden during the 2000–15 period. The acceptance of dual citizenship, the introduction of citizenship ceremonies, and the increasing focus on labour immigration over the past decade represent concrete examples of the Canadian inspiration.

Towards Mutual Inspiration and Policy Convergence?

Immigration and integration policy transfer from Canada to Sweden in forms of both emulation and inspiration has unfolded over the entire 2000–15 time period and should be seen as an iterative process rather than as a single, discrete event at a specific point in time. This extended time frame has the potential of capturing learning dynamics characterized by long lags and complex causal chains. In particular, the extended period allows for an evaluation of mutual adaptation, co-evolution, and policy convergence across countries, whereby policy convergence is seen as a process of "becoming" rather than a condition of "being" more alike.[61]

The growing Swedish fascination with the Canadian immigration and integration policy model has clearly resulted in increased contacts among Canadian and Swedish officials and politicians in both bilateral and multilateral settings. Although often initiated by Sweden, this process has also contributed to increased understanding and knowledge about Swedish policies and practices among Canadian officials and politicians. A senior official from Citizenship and Immigration Canada confirmed as much: "We have actually been learning a bit from the Swedes, because certainly in the last number of years, I think the Swedes have almost leapfrogged ahead of Canada on some of their policies, particularly as it pertains to employer flexibility and employer freedom to bring in foreign workers."[62] The reference is here to the law on labour immigration that was adopted in 2008, which has led academics to refer to Sweden as "the world's most open country."[63]

The impression of recent increased awareness of and interest in Swedish immigration and integration policies in Canada is further supported by a September 2015 study trip to Sweden by the Leaders' Roundtable on Immigration, which is an executive network convened by the Conference Board of Canada, a Canadian not-for-profit think tank dedicated to researching and analysing public policy issues. The Leaders' Roundtable on Immigration includes as members, among other public and private stakeholders, government leaders and officials in the citizenship and immigration sector, and it is designed to champion immigration-related issues that are important to Canada's future prosperity. Several representatives from provincial and federal ministries of citizenship and immigration were in the Canadian delegation to Sweden that counted more than twenty participants. The main purpose of the study trip was to assess the extent to which "Sweden's experience in handling a high intake of refugees may contain lessons for Canada – in particular, understanding how Sweden values the human capital and skills they bring."[64] More specific learning objectives were also stated in the detailed and comprehensive study-trip program:

- to gain insight into the immigration context in Sweden and to exchange expertise between Canadian and Swedish immigration leaders;
- to explore Sweden's experience of welcoming and integrating immigrants and refugees into the labour market;
- to exchange perspectives on immigration issues, in particular, to learn how Sweden values the human capital that refugees bring and works to engage them in the economy;
- to showcase Canada's expertise and leadership in immigration; and
- to inform the development of a National Immigration Action Plan for Canada.

During the week in Sweden, the Leaders' Roundtable on Immigration met with a wide range of Swedish representatives, including members of Parliament, central and local government officials, business leaders, immigration policy experts, and practitioners in different sectors. The expectation for these meetings was that "discussions between Canadian and Swedish leaders will result in shared lessons, which could help inform new programs or adjust existing ones."[65] Furthermore, the Conference Board of Canada intended to officially evaluate and publish the insights gained from the trip to Sweden in a separate report. Potential lessons for Canada would also be discussed in future seminars and workshops. The initial impressions were very positive. According to a high-ranking representative from the Conference Board of Canada, the study trip to Sweden "exceeded our expectations."[66]

Visits from Canadian immigration and integration stakeholders to Sweden have until now been a rarity. According to an official at the Embassy of Canada to Sweden, this was the first time, during his three-decades-long tenure at the embassy, that a Canadian delegation with an explicit focus on Swedish immigration and integration policy had visited Sweden.[67] The increased awareness of each other's policies and practices within the field of immigration control and immigrant integration may lead to the formation of collective identities and shared understandings among policy actors in both nations. This view is supported by high-ranking Swedish civil servants, one of whom asserted that Canada and Sweden have increasingly "found each other" in matters of immigration and integration policy over the years due to Sweden's opposition to common European trends towards increasingly closed borders and scepticism of multiculturalism.[68]

Bevelander and Pendakur have also grasped this apparent mutual policy attraction in their study of labour market integration of refugees and family reunion immigrants in Canada and Sweden:

In the Swedish debate, Canada is often identified as an important positive example of a country where immigrants from all over the world integrate largely without problems. In the Canadian debate, Sweden's integration policies are held up as the gold standard for facilitating positive social and economic outcomes, but not something that the Canadian state is willing to match. The situation is complicated by the fact that Canada and Sweden have different intake levels and concentrate on different categories of migrants.[69]

Their observations pinpoint a key finding: countries may look for and find inspiration abroad despite different domestic circumstances and without the intention to copy or emulate other policy models directly and completely. This description seems to capture the nature of the role that the Canadian immigration and integration policy model played in the Swedish reform process between 2000 and 2015. Increasingly, this logic may also explain the growing interest in Swedish policies and practices in Canada.

It remains to be seen whether Canada's and Sweden's mutual inspiration will continue. Recent events demonstrate the unpredictability associated with the politics of migration. While Canada initially took a cautious and hesitant approach to the refugee crisis that struck Europe in 2015, Sweden was – along with Germany – among the earliest and most welcoming countries for the refugees. The new Liberal government that assumed office in Canada in November 2015, however, caused a radical shift in the Canadian position by pledging to accept 25,000 Syrian refugees by the end of the year. At the same time, after asylum seekers began arriving on Swedish soil at a rate of 10,000 per week, and official estimates indicated that 190,000 asylum seekers in total could arrive in 2015, the Swedish prime minister declared, in November, that the country's generous asylum regime would end: "It pains me that Sweden is no longer capable of receiving asylum seekers at the high level we do today. We simply cannot do any more."[70] This policy statement led to the adoption of a number of restrictive legislative changes in 2016. For instance, those who have applied for asylum and received a deportation order will no longer have the right to accommodation or a daily allowance from Swedish authorities. Furthermore, the possibility of asylum seekers obtaining a residence permit and reuniting with their families was limited.[71]

Despite persistent differences in both policy priorities and practices, a special relationship between Canada and Sweden has emerged in the area of immigration and integration policy since the early 2000s. This relationship is based on regular and frequent contacts and interactions, over an extended period of time, between Canadian and Swedish politicians and civil servants. The enduring policy dialogue that has resulted embodies signs of mutual inspiration, adaptation, and the coevolution of policies. The relationship between Canada and Sweden is perhaps the best illustration of what Keith Banting refers to as the emerging "transatlantic convergence" between Canada and Europe.[72]

Denmark's Selective Political Attention: The Development of an Alternative Model

Canadian experiences have been incorporated in Danish politics, but in modified form. Primarily the points-based system and the hosting programs have been incorporated but, of course, in modified forms ... The way things are done in Denmark is very different from in Canada.

High-ranking Danish civil servant[1]

In stark contrast to the Swedish case, immigration and integration policies were highly politicized issues in Denmark during the 1990s and early 2000s.[2] In fact, these issues completely dominated the campaign leading to the local and national elections in November 2001. After the elections, the new Liberal/Conservative coalition government set out to drastically reform Danish immigration and integration policies. Its main objectives were to further restrict access to the nation for some types of immigrants and to accelerate the integration of those already residing legally in Denmark. Østergaard-Nielsen succinctly describes the initiatives: "The message from the right-wing parties was clear: it must be more difficult to migrate to Denmark, more difficult to stay, and if migrants stay, they have to learn Danish, work, and in general 'fit in' and contribute to Danish society."[3]

The new government acted with exceptional speed. A comprehensive proposal for a new immigration policy was presented in January 2002.[4] Just two months later, the government followed up with a proposal for a new integration policy.[5] Following the presentation of these proposals, a status report on the reformed Danish immigration and integration policies was presented in early 2003,[6] and an action plan was launched in 2005.[7]

Increased Politicization and Radical Reforms

The reforms introduced by the new Danish government after 2001 established a more selective immigration policy.[8] The rules on economic immigration were liberalized while regulations for family immigration became increasingly restrictive. For instance, although family reunification was still possible, the *legal* claim to it was revoked. The introduction of the controversial "24-year rule," which states that a foreign spouse can only be admitted if both spouses are at least twenty-four years of age, illustrates this trend. Family reunification was further restricted by increased emphasis on national attachment and new regulations on financial assistance and accommodation requirements. The new rules provided for family reunification only if a married couple had a national attachment to Denmark considered to be *greater* than their attachment to any other country. According to Danish law, the national attachment requirement does not apply to those who have been Danish citizens for twenty-six years or more. This rule has been under attack since the Strasbourg-based European Court of Human Rights declared in 2016 that the law discriminates against people who are born outside of Denmark and who seek to obtain Danish citizenship later in life. It also became more difficult to obtain refugee status in Denmark. With a view to restrict the number of recognized refugees, the "Aliens Package" abolished the de facto concept under section 7(2) of the Aliens Act, so that residence permits would only be granted to asylum seekers eligible for protection in Denmark according to the international conventions.[9] Furthermore, the government introduced new practices to accelerate the deportation process for rejected asylum seekers.

The implementation of a more selective immigration policy strategy after 2001 had major practical implications. While the total number of immigrants to Denmark grew, the number of both refugees and family immigrants fell drastically. Whereas 6,499 spouses came to Denmark through family reunification in 2001, the number dropped to 2,619 in 2008.[10] According to Rytter, the most frequent reason for newly-wed couples, consisting of a Dane and a foreign spouse, to be denied reunification is that their combined national attachment to Denmark – a subjective calculation made by the immigration authorities – is considered insufficient.[11] The overall increase in immigration to Denmark during this period was due to the admission of significantly higher numbers of economic immigrants and students. In 2000, only 25 per cent of residence permits were issued to people from non-Western countries for employment or education purposes. By 2008, the share of residence permits granted for such purposes had reached 80 per cent for the same groups. This significant change was associated with an upward trend in employment rates so that the gap between the rates of native Danes and non-Western immigrants fell from 33 to 23 percentage points between 2000 and 2008.[12] The employment rate gap increased slightly after the recession in 2008, and was about 26 percentage points between 2010 and 2013.[13] Comprehensive, high-spending, income-tax-financed welfare states require high average employment rates to be sustainable, and it is clear that the future of the welfare state was a central justification for the new immigration policy. As will be demonstrated, the Canadian model was an important inspiration for the renewed focus on labour immigration.

In terms of immigrant integration, however, Danish reforms during the reassessment phase advanced an assimilationist, as opposed to a Canadian-style multiculturalist, approach. Denmark never adopted an official multiculturalism policy. Indeed, anti-multiculturalism has dominated the public discourse. The tendency has been that "'the national' or 'the Danish' has been given a far more central position."[14] This trend began with the 1998 Integration Act and was reinforced after the 2001 election. According to Lægaard, "anti-multiculturalism was a de facto reigning ideology from 2001" in Denmark.[15] For instance, compulsory integration programs for refugees and family immigrants and a special integration benefit that was considerably lower than social assistance rates were introduced. Although Denmark opened for dual citizenship in 2014, a series of measures introduced during the 2000–15 period made it more difficult to become a permanent resident and Danish citizen.[16] The requirements for obtaining permanent residency were initially raised to seven years.[17] Thus in theory, refugees could be deported if the conflict in their country of origin was resolved within the seven-year period. Reunified family members who were divorced within this period would similarly not be guaranteed permission to remain in Denmark.[18] In addition, residency requirements for Danish citizenship were raised from seven to nine years. Moreover, prospective citizens must not have received social assistance benefits for more than one of the preceding five years and must also demonstrate knowledge of the Danish language and society by passing a citizenship test.

Over the past decade, Denmark has also introduced reforms to make the welfare state less inclusive for immigrants than before. For instance, Denmark implemented a system in which the level of social assistance benefits a person would receive was dependent on the time the applicant had spent on Danish territory.[19] Although not formally directed towards immigrants, the reduced Start Help benefit, the "apron circular" policy that was intended to increase work incentives in instances where both husband and wife were outside the labour market, and the 300/450-hour rule that required occupational employment for a predetermined number of hours to be eligible to receive cash benefits all seemed to affect immigrants to a greater extent than the majority population.[20]

The centre-left government that replaced the Liberal/ Conservative government in 2011 initiated several changes to Danish immigration and integration policies, notably advancing a more open and accommodating rhetoric towards immigrants.[21] However, overall since 2001, Denmark has progressively implemented a more selective immigration strategy along with an increasingly assimilationist approach to immigrant integration. Judging by its reaction to the European refugee crisis, this trend is likely to continue under the new centre-right minority government that assumed office after the 2015 election. In the early stages of the crisis, the Danish government published a letter informing the world that it had decided to tighten regulations concerning refugees in a number of areas.[22] The letter, which was initially published in Arabic and English in four Lebanese newspapers and is now available on the Danish government's website in a number of strategically selected languages (Albanian, Arabic, Danish, English, Farsi, Pashto, Russian, Serbian, Somali, and Tigrinya), is worth quoting at length:

> The Danish Parliament has just passed a regulation to:
> - Reduce the social benefits significantly. The social benefits for newly arrived refugees will be reduced by up to 50 per cent.
>
> The government will maintain and ensure that:
> - Foreign nationals, granted temporary protection in Denmark, will not have the right to bring family members to Denmark during the first year.
> - Foreign nationals can only be granted a permanent residence permit after 5 years at the earliest. Prior to this, they risk having their residence permit revoked.
> - In order to obtain a permanent residence permit in Denmark, there are language requirements in terms of the ability to speak and understand the Danish language.

- When an application for asylum is regarded manifestly unfounded, it is refused in accordance with a particularly expedited procedure.
- All rejected asylum seekers must be returned quickly from Denmark.
- There is a special return centre to ensure that rejected asylum seekers leave Denmark as quickly as possible."[23]

This letter, which was actually an advertisement aimed at deterring refugees from arriving in the country, has been followed by other controversial policies. The proposal to confiscate valuables of refugees and asylum seekers worth more than 10,000 kroner (approximately $2,000 CAD) to cover costs for their food and housing was met with massive international attention. Principles endemic to the Danish welfare state were evoked as justification, as explained by a member of Parliament from the governing Liberal Party: "A prerequisite for this universal welfare state is the fundamental principle that when you live in Denmark, if you are able to pay for your own food and housing, you should do so. If not, the government will provide this for you. This applies to Danes, and with this bill, it will also apply to refugees coming to Denmark. I believe this is a fair and balanced approach – to align services and obligations as we do to people born here."[24]

The objective of ensuring the future of the comparatively very generous Danish welfare state is key to understanding Denmark's approach to immigration control and immigrant integration during the 2000–15 period. It is here interesting to note that, overall, the welfare state generosity in Denmark during this reassessment phase was significantly higher than that in Sweden.[25] This factor may explain the divergent paths towards immigration and integration policy taken by the two Scandinavian neighbours.

Canada has been a central reference in the Danish reform debate and process. However, the Danish approach to the Canadian immigration and integration policy model is complex. While expert inquiry commissions devoted substantial attention to the Canadian model by systematically analysing its advantages and disadvantages in the Danish context, more selective and fragmented attention came from the political level. Among politicians, the Canadian model was in some areas employed actively as a mythical model and a symbol of success to legitimize changes in Danish policies and practices. In other areas, the Canadian model was ignored or outright rejected, and the focus of discussion was instead devoted to finding *Danish* solutions to *Danish* realities. In other words, Danish reformers did not take an all-encompassing approach to the Canadian model as a complete package of administrative reforms. For sure, the deeply entwined relationship between the policies on immigration control and immigrant integration, integral to the Canadian model, was disregarded in Denmark. Accordingly, there is a contradiction in Denmark between the objective of attracting labour immigrants and the privileges granted to landed immigrants. Their restricted access to family reunification and the complicated and lengthy citizenship process are indicative. This contradiction reflects politicians' selective "pick-and-choose" use of social science research in reforming Danish immigration and integration policies since the early 2000s.[26]

Selective Political Attention to the Canadian Model: Towards a New National Model

The Canadian immigration and integration model is well known in Denmark and was subject to considerable scrutiny towards the end of the 1990s and early 2000s. Both the Social Democratic ministers of interior, Birte Weiss (1993 to 1997) and Karen Jespersen (2000 to 2001), embarked on study trips to Canada.[27] Upon her return from Canada in 1997, Weiss declared that there were important lessons to be learned for Denmark: "It was striking that in Canada the main thing is that people should be self-helped. It is the main theme in their integration efforts. People should have a job so they can contribute to society. It is all about people becoming contributors to Canadian society as swiftly as possible and not receivers."[28] Weiss was obviously referring to the notion of immigrants as a resource for the country, which is a central element of the carefully managed approach to immigration in Canada.

In 2015, Weiss vividly recalled her study trip to Canada almost twenty years earlier as "inspirational."[29] However, at the time, a high-ranking civil servant who also participated in the study trip warned against using the Canadian system in Denmark due to the significant differences between the two countries with respect to immigration histories and traditions.[30] Nevertheless, Canada clearly served as a source of inspiration in the process that led to the adoption of the 1998 Integration Act, with its emphasis on self-sufficiency and individual responsibility as means of integration, according to one high-ranking civil servant.[31] Another senior civil servant argued with reference to the potential tension between immigration and the welfare state that the introduction of the short-lived, special integration benefit for immigrants, lower than the standard cash benefit for social assistance, was inspired by Danish interpretations of Canadian realities.[32] The interviewee alleged a similar "mindset" between the two countries in that sponsored family class immigrants to Canada are also ineligible for social assistance for the duration of the sponsorship period.

However, the Canadian model disappeared from the political agenda in the immediate aftermath of the 2001 election. The reforms initiated by the new government between 2001 and 2005 represented a sharp break with the past and were motivated by a purely "national agenda." In particular, the growing popularity of the populist and anti-immigrant Danish People's Party pushed the established parties towards restrictive reforms. The concept of "Danishness," often juxtaposed with "un-Danishness," dominated the political debate.[33] In this disputatious political climate, the Canadian model – or other foreign models, for that matter – did not play a crucial role in the debate. In fact, the Danish government considered itself to be an international innovator in the area of immigration and integration policy reform. The new controversial policies on family reunification were proudly presented and described by the government as "the strictest in the world" when they were introduced in 2002.[34] Then minister of integration, Bertel Haarder, boasted, "I am certain that many countries will follow our example in the years to come. Denmark can be considered a pioneer in this area."[35]

Denmark has, indeed, introduced a number of innovative policies and practices in both immigration control and immigrant integration since the early 2000s, and some of these initiatives have been adopted by other countries. For instance, some governments, including the Norwegian, have recently repeated Denmark's practice of placing advertisements in foreign newspapers in order to discourage and deter refugees from seeking asylum in the country. However novel, Danish policies and practices have also been strongly condemned by other countries and international organizations. The controversial twenty-four-year rule is a prime example. The labour and immigration ministers from Belgium, France, and Sweden declared in an open letter to the Danish government that they did not intend to follow Denmark's lead.[36] A highly critical report from the Council of Europe's Commissioner for Human Rights was also tabled in 2004.[37] The commissioner recommended that the twenty-four-year provision on family reunification be reconsidered. The Danish government, in response, defended the rule as a measure aimed at "avoiding forced marriages and arranged marriages and thereby protecting young people."[38] A prominent member of Parliament for the governing party in 2008 argued that the measure would prevent un-Danish behaviour: "Now we are doubling the penalty for forced marriages. We want to send an unambiguous signal to those immigrant communities who still practice this primitive, un-Danish form of marriage."[39]

Despite the government's focus on the "national," other Danish groups made active references to international solutions, including the Canadian immigration and integration policy model. Both the Think Tank on Integration (Tænketanken om utfordringer for integrationsindsatsen i Danmark) and the Welfare Commission (Velfærdskommissionen), which were appointed in 2000 and 2003, respectively, emphasized the importance of analysing international experiences in immigration and integration policy. Canada's model received substantial attention from both expert commissions.[40]

The five-member Think Tank on Integration, which was appointed by Social-Democratic minister of interior Karen Jespersen, included two university professors and three civil servants. In 2001, the Think Tank published its first report on the integration of immigrants into Danish society. A year later, a second report on probable demographic developments was published. The third report, also published in 2002, considered the economic consequences of demographic developments and the integration of immigrants. The objective of the fourth report was to describe and compare Denmark's immigration and integration policies with those of seven selected Western countries and to clarify "what and how much Denmark can learn from these countries."[41] In this report, published in 2004, the Think Tank presented an ambivalent view on the relevance of the Canadian model:

> The strategy differing most radically from the Danish one is found in Canada. In Canada they combine a fairly easy immigration policy with very low cash benefits. It is entirely unrealistic to combine such policy with the kind of welfare model that seems to find support in Denmark. It might, however, be possible to gain inspiration from the Canadian tradition of a strong voluntary and popular involvement in the efforts to integrate into society newly arrived refugees and persons reunified with their family. Greater mutual openness for everyday contact is presumed to be one of the most essential conditions for improved integration.[42]

In the longer Danish version of the report, which was based on a comprehensive background study produced by the Danish National Centre for Social Research (SFI),[43] the same message was presented, drawing upon several of the theoretical concepts pertaining to policy transfer and learning discussed previously: "Although we in Denmark cannot nor wish to *transfer* the entire Canadian integration model to the Danish welfare state, Denmark can *learn* from Canada. Denmark can, among other things, draw *inspiration* from the Canadian tradition."[44] The Think Tank concluded by conceding that it had been swayed by the Canadian model: "Denmark should promote voluntary work aiming to build personal contacts between Danes and newly arrived refugees and immigrants, e.g., by allocating a voluntary personal host to them. This scheme has been inspired by Canadian programmes."[45]

Although many Danish municipalities have implemented host programs to help settle new immigrants, these programs did not engender much attention among politicians during the 2000s. Instead, they chose to focus on the objective of restricting immigration to the country, in particular family immigrants. However, a more open approach was adopted for labour immigration during this period. The Think Tank on Integration proposed a points-based system to make highly qualified foreigners eligible for temporary residence permits in order to seek employment in Denmark. This proposal was explicitly "inspired by the Canadian rating system, which governs the economic immigration to the country."[46]

Concerns about the future of the welfare state have been fundamental to Danish discourse on immigration and integration policy, which is a reason why the Canadian "points system" has been promoted. The Welfare Commission, comprised of nine members (including four academic researchers, three representatives from the private business sector, and two representatives from non-governmental organizations), was appointed by the Liberal/Conservative government to identify and address future challenges facing the Danish welfare state system. In its extensive deliberations on immigration and integration, the commission singled out Canada as a special case because its immigration policy is "directed towards fulfilling the needs of the labour market for specific qualifications."[47] The Canadian "points system" was highlighted: "Canada has in contrast to the remaining countries a long tradition of economic immigration and gives access to skilled workers based on a special points system."[48] Then, in its final report published in 2005, the Welfare Commission proposed the introduction of a points system for labour immigrants, inspired by the Canadian system.[49]

Representatives from various industry and business groups in Denmark have been very active and influential in both raising awareness of and advocating for the implementation of a points system for labour immigrants.[50] For instance, in the official hearings and deliberations on the Welfare Commission's proposals, the Confederation of Danish Employers, the Confederation of Danish Industry, the Danish Federation of Trade and Service, the Danish Agricultural Council, and the Danish Bankers Association actively supported what was referred to as a "Canadian-inspired points system to attract immigrants with better qualifications."[51] The Canadian system was in this respect seen as a tool to ensure the future of the Danish welfare state.

Based upon the proposals from the Think Tank on Integration and the Welfare Commission, a new Green-card scheme for labour immigrants was launched in Denmark in 2007. Despite several modifications over the years, the scheme was still in effect at the time of writing. The system is similar to its Canadian counterpart. The resemblances are not surprising because leading Danish politicians early on expressed the intention to "copy/paste" the Canadian system.[52] To be granted a resident permit under the Danish Green-card scheme, applicants must obtain a minimum of 100 points, with points earned for educational level (maximum 130 points), language skills (maximum 40 points), and "adaptability" (maximum 15 points). Furthermore, individual applicants must be able to document an ability to support themselves financially during their first year in Denmark.

Although the Danish points system was inspired by the Canadian system, the two systems vary on several accounts. The definition and allocation of "adaptability" points are, for instance, different. In Denmark, adaptability points are based on previous educational or work-related attachments to the European Union, the European Economic Area, or Switzerland. Such attachments are perceived to increase an applicant's ability to quickly adapt to the Danish labour market. This criterion implies that education and work-related experience in these thirty-two countries count more than equivalent experience elsewhere. Adaptability in the Canadian system is confined to the relationship with Canada, with points awarded based on the applicant's (or spouse or partner's) previous education and work experience in Canada, whether relatives live in Canada, whether employment has been arranged, and the spouse or partner's language competencies in English or French.

The Danish government, unlike its Canadian counterpart, extended the points system to family reunifications in 2010. Foreign-resident spouses could qualify for family reunification through "integration-relevant qualifications" such as language competence, education level and education institution, career field, and work experience.[53] The 2010 changes significantly reduced the number of labour immigration applications as well as the proportion of accepted applications from those who applied.[54] Although the extension of the points system to family reunification followed the expert advice of the Welfare Commission, the Think Tank on Integration proposed a points-based system for economic immigrants more in line with the original Canadian system. The proposals from the two expert groups were based on fundamentally different reasoning. As one representative who was involved in the work of both entities put it: "[The points system for family reunification] was all about limiting the number of new immigrants, while the points system as suggested by the Think Tank was all about making it more easy for qualified persons to come to Denmark."[55] However, the centre-left government that assumed office after the 2011 election was quick to repeal the use of the points system for family reunifications. Although inspired by the Canadian system, the Danish points system for labour immigration demonstrates how an external national model can be adapted and reproduced in a new context.

Other elements of the Canadian immigration and integration policy model have been completely rejected in Denmark. Canadian integration policies and multicultural thinking in which cultural diversity is valued and group identities are given more-or-less formal recognition have not received much support in Denmark during the past decade. Denmark and Canada are often portrayed as polar opposites in regard to multiculturalism.[56] While Canada scored 7.5 out of 8 on the Multiculturalism Policy Index in 2000 and 2010 – the highest score among twenty-one OECD countries – Denmark fell from 0.5 to 0.0 during the same period.[57] Although both countries require immigrants to pass a citizenship test to be naturalized, the Danish test, with its focus on national history, achievements, and heroes of various types, has a clear ethnic orientation. Canada's civic-oriented test, by contrast, predominantly consists of questions regarding political institutions, rights and responsibilities, and political values.[58] In his study of naturalization practices among a group of twenty-six countries, Koning places Canada and Denmark at opposite ends of the spectrum.[59] Weide claims that in Canada, naturalization is understood as contributing to the integration process, whereas in the Danish system, "entry, stay, and naturalization were during the 2000s viewed as prizes to be granted to the most deserving," that is, the most integrated.[60] In Denmark, the naturalization test consists of multiple-choice questions, and the passing score is 32/40. In December 2011, 70.4 per cent of the applicants passed the test.[61] The difficulty of the test prompted Ersbøll, in a chapter with the illustrative title "On Trial in Denmark," to claim that "future citizens have to do better than the average Danish citizen in order to become a member of the Danish citizenry."[62]

The Muhammad cartoon controversy in 2005 and 2006 was regarded by many as an expression of the tensions in attitudes towards multiculturalism in Denmark. Following his appointment as minister of integration in March 2011, Søren Pind openly denounced multiculturalism in an article, proclaiming that "the multicultural society is recognizable as a parallel society where people isolate against and away from each other, and where cultures and norms, which are distant from the Danish, thrive."[63] In a recent newspaper article, another high-profile minister in several governments of the 1990s and 2000s, Karen Jespersen – who also embarked on study trip to Canada – openly criticizes the Canadian model.[64] Referring to several unspecified surveys, Jespersen and her coauthor give the impression that multiculturalism is increasingly unpopular among Canadians and that Canada therefore has become "a wet blanket in the face of the politically correct multicultural dreamers" in Denmark.[65]

During interviews, Danish politicians and senior-level civil servants fully recognized the distinctiveness of the Canadian immigration and integration policy model. However, the model was not perceived as an "all-or-nothing" solution to Danish challenges. Throughout the Danish reform process, various components of the Canadian model received selective attention from both elected officials and expert commissions. Although it was widely regarded as a successful model, the relationship between the Canadian model and Denmark can best be described in terms of soft policy transfer where the Canadian model inspired fresh thinking about policy challenges and helped in facilitating policy changes. In cases where basic ideas behind Canadian programs actually were adopted – like the Canadian-style points system for immigration – the programs were adjusted and adapted, sometimes fundamentally, to Danish realities. Non-transfer was also documented. The Danish approach to immigrant integration, based on coercive and assimilative policies, is antithetical to the Canadian model.[66] The deeply entwined relationship between the policies on immigration control (open and expansive) and immigrant integration (inclusive multiculturalist), a defining characteristic of the Canadian model, is therefore completely absent in Denmark.

The Declining Role of Outside Expertise in the
Danish Reform Process

In order to understand the relationship of the Canadian model to immigration and integration policy reforms in Denmark between 2000 and 2015, the role of expert knowledge in Danish policy-making requires consideration. In general, the speed in which the sweeping reforms of Danish immigration and integration policies were introduced in the close aftermath of the 2001 election is an indication of the merely symbolic role that scientific expertise and research played in this process.

Expert inquiry commissions have traditionally constituted an institutionalized mechanism for pre-legislative consultation between the executive and relevant policy actors in the gestation of public policy in Scandinavia. However, the reform of Danish immigration and integration policies during the 2000s represented a break with this tradition. White papers or related specialized reports were abandoned, more often than not, when dealing with immigration and/or integration in Denmark during the period. The last white paper addressing such issues was published in 1998.[67] Commenting on the decreasing use of white papers in the area of immigration and integration policy, one high-ranking Danish civil servant contends that "the pace has increased. One does not have time to wait for large-scale inquiries anymore."[68]

The divorce of social science research and scientific expertise from policy-making can be traced back to the former Danish prime minister, Anders Fogh Rasussen. In his New Year Speech shortly after entering office in 2001, he proclaimed:

We do not need experts and arbiters of taste to decide on our behalf. In recent years, a veritable wilderness of governmental councils and committees and institutions has shot up everywhere. Many of them have developed into state-authorized arbiters of taste who lay down the law as to what is right and wrong in various areas. There is a tendency towards a tyranny of experts, which runs the risk of suppressing free popular debate. The Danish population must not accept admonishing fingers from so-called experts who think they know best. Experts are fine when it comes to conveying actual knowledge. But when it comes to making personal choices, all of us are experts. The government will eliminate superfluous councils, committees, and institutions. It will be a comprehensive clean-up.[69]

Martin Bak Jørgensen states that in Denmark the research-policy relationship can best be represented as a "pick-and-choose" model where politicians and policy-makers employ research that supports the prevailing perception of integration and definition of problems; research thereby serves a legitimizing function.[70] For instance, it is alleged that the comprehensive research presented by the Think Tank on Integration was not used instrumentally, but rather symbolically, to legitimize government policies already defined and implemented.[71] A member of the Think Tank confirmed that there was a tendency for politicians to increasingly seek "shorter and quicker answers" to questions related to actual, concrete policies rather than to seek the longer and more comprehensive background reports that addressed issues and questions identified and selected by the Think Tank itself.[72] The member characterized the new trend as a change in requests for "thorough technical/professional advice" to "politically oriented advice."[73] The Think Tank was terminated in March 2007 and replaced in 2008 by the Inter-Ministerial Working Group for Better Integration.[74] The new working group consisted solely of representatives from various (seven) government ministries, signifying that the role of outside expertise had been diminished further.

The declining role of outside research and expertise in the Danish reform process has been contrasted with the situation in Sweden where ad hoc expert commissions significantly shaped the immigration and integration policy reform process during the 2000s. Study tours to Canada formed an integral part of the scientific approach adopted in Sweden. Representatives from Citizenship and Immigration Canada (CIC) confirm that there had been significantly less interest in the Canadian model from Danish politicians and civil servants during the same period.[75] Representatives from the Embassy of Denmark in Ottawa agree with this impression.[76] Extensive politicization is one important explanation for the declining role of outside research and expert knowledge in Danish immigration and integration policy-making since the early 2000s.[77] In the context of strong political mobilization, international policy models tend to be used more for symbolic reasons rather than for instrumental purposes. The Danish case supports this contention.

Chapter Four

Norway's Inspired but Still Slow Learning: A Reluctant Reformer

The first thing one thinks about is that Canada is viewed as a country that welcomes [immigrants] with open arms and that has an interesting integration policy. Yes, Canada is interesting and we need to acquire more knowledge about it.

High-ranking Norwegian civil servant[1]

While sweeping immigration and integration policy reforms were introduced in Denmark and Sweden during the 2000s, Norway was also reassessing its policies and actively searching for new solutions. But Norway did so without committing to the same level of comprehensive reforms as Denmark and Sweden. This finding corresponds well with the image of Norway as a "slow learner" or "reluctant reformer" in relation to public policy developments.[2] Norway is still in the midst of an ongoing reassessment phase on immigration and integration policy much like Denmark and Sweden. Nevertheless, between 2000 and 2015 substantial attention was paid to the Canadian immigration and integration policy model by media, expert commissions, civil servants, and politicians. In particular, and unlike in Denmark, the role of experts in this reassessment phase has been significant. The lack of comprehensive reforms in Norway is largely attributable to their role.

Canadian Inspiration

The modern political history of Norway has been characterized by "peaceful coexistence and revolution in slow motion."[3] The modern Norwegian welfare state, which combines solid financial growth, high employment rates, and comprehensive universal welfare programs with a relatively even distribution of income, was built without agonizing conflicts. Significantly, expert commissions have played a central role in advancing this "revolution" and in sustaining Norway's stability.

A reliance on experts was identified early as an important factor in contributing to the successful development of the Scandinavian nations.[4] American political scientist Thomas Anton, analysing Swedish policy-making in the late 1960s, contends that the extensive use of commissions contributed to a "politics as work" rather than to a "politics as game" ethic, and to a "problem-focused" rather than "theory-focused" orientation.[5] The use of expert inquiry commissions in Scandinavia has constituted an institutionalized mechanism for pre-legislative consultation among the executive and relevant policy actors in the development of public policy. The consultative tradition has especially long roots in Norway where it predates the emergence of political parties and mass politics.[6] According to Arter, there were around 894 commissions at work between 1814 and 1900 in Norway, or on average about ten new ones annually.[7] The figure rose to twenty new commissions annually between 1900 and 1936. However, the real expansion of the expert commission system coincided with the increased role of the state in social and economic management after the Second World War. During the 1970s, more than 1,000 Norwegian commissions were at work at any given time.[8] However, the number of commissions has decreased some since the 1980s. At the end of 2000, 477 permanent and 66 temporary commissions were at work.[9] More importantly, expert commissions have played a key role in the recent debate on immigration and welfare in Norway.

The Immigration Law Committee (Utlendingslovsutvalget), which was established in 2001 and delivered its report in 2004, was mandated to prepare a proposal for a new Immigration Act.[10] During the committee hearings and deliberations, the Norwegian Parliament instructed the government in May 2005 to study the possibility of adopting a new sponsorship system for family reunifications in the case of spouses. The Canadian model played a key role in the proposal: "Based on the Canadian model, a three-year sponsorship system should be evaluated for those who bring their spouse to Norway from another country. This implies that the resident is responsible economically to the state if the person coming to Norway is in need of social support from the public during the first three years of residence."[11] In addition, a minority group of members of Parliament proposed that "as in Canada, persons who marry a permanent resident and have been granted family reunification should be granted permanent residency immediately."[12]

The government followed up on these requests and asked for an opinion from the Directorate of Immigration (UDI), the central agency in the immigration administration in Norway. In its reply, the UDI warned against applying a fragment of an external policy model to Norwegian realities. The warning specifically touched on central themes pertaining to policy transfer and learning across borders, and so is worth quoting:

> The proposal refers to the Canadian model for family immigration. This model can, however, not be evaluated independent of general immigration policies adopted in Canada. With an extensive use of "sponsorship," the Canadian authorities have based their laws and immigration policies on a completely different philosophy than the Norwegian authorities. Introducing sponsorship would imply that the Norwegian authorities would select a fragment of the Canadian system. The question can be raised whether this fragment will be compatible with current principles for family immigration, based on today's and proposed immigration legislation. Using the Canadian model as a reference requires more comprehensive studies of Canadian immigration policies and the Canadian welfare system.[13]

During the Immigration Law Committee hearings and deliberations, a minority group also requested the Norwegian government to involve more actors in the immigrant integration work. Again, Canada served as inspiration: "Voluntary organizations and municipalities should be granted economic resources, based on the Canadian model, to organize projects for those immigrant groups that are not covered by the Introductory Act in order to guide them in the Norwegian society, help them to transfer their education and competencies to the Norwegian context and be a point of support in the integration process."[14]

The Canadian model ultimately became subject to more systematic attention from the Welfare and Migration Committee (Velferds- og migrasjonsutvalget) that was established in 2009 and delivered its report in 2011.[15] The mandate of this expert committee was to describe and assess, in detail, elements of the Norwegian welfare model that influence and are influenced by increasing migration. The committee was also required to adopt a comparative perspective, and so five countries were chosen for special attention: Canada, Denmark, the Netherlands, Sweden, and the United States. Thus immigration and integration policies in other countries of Europe and elsewhere received attention in this Scandinavian reassessment phase. The choice of Canada was natural since the attention given to the Canadian immigration and integration policy model had increased significantly in Norway during the 2000s. In addition to the numerous references to Canada in the report, the committee commissioned Canadian academic and immigration expert Keith Banting to write a twenty-page account of the Canadian model to be incorporated into the final report.[16] Apparently, the committee sought to rely directly on Canadian expertise rather than exclusively on its own analytic deliberations from afar.[17]

Based on Canada's experiences with multiculturalism as an official government policy, the Inclusion Committee (Inkluderingsutvalget), established in 2010, also devoted special attention to the Canadian model in its discussion of challenges and proposals for a multicultural Norway.[18]

In addition to these three ad hoc expert commissions, the Canadian model received direct consideration from politicians in Norway during the reassessment phase. For instance, a study trip to Canada formed an important background for the White Paper on Diversity that was presented in 2004.[19] A high-profile delegation, including the minister holding the immigration and integration policy portfolio in the Norwegian government, Erna Solberg, spent nearly a week in Canada in July 2003. A participant on this trip claims that, in general, the visit was a positive learning experience. In particular, this high-ranking civil servant – based on the contrary situation in Norway – was struck by the normalcy of being an immigrant and speaking with an accent in Canada: "It is a trivial fact that they come from many different countries."[20] Although it is fully understood that "Norway and Canada have very different immigration histories and that experiences cannot be directly transferred," the white paper emphasizes that

> Canada has a fundamentally positive attitude towards immigration that the government feels Norway can learn from. Through both political and symbolic actions, the Canadian authorities emphasize inclusion. "We who live in Canada" includes everybody with legal residency. The country views the inclusion of new immigrant groups in the system of public goods and services as a natural aspect of politics and societal development. At the same time, the authorities are clear on what constitutes common Canadian values and the importance of learning the official languages, English or French. The government is of the opinion that Canada can give Norway important *inspiration* through the manner in which a positive and inclusive attitude towards immigration is combined with clear demands and expectations.[21]

The White Paper on Diversity must be seen in relation to the Introductory Act, which became effective in 2004.[22] This was Norway's first law on immigrant integration. Although important for formalizing individual rights and obligations for various categories of immigrants, many practical questions related to immigrant integration were not addressed in the act. The question of citizenship was, for example, addressed in a separate citizenship bill, approved in 2005.[23] This bill was based on the recommendations of yet another expert inquiry commission that delivered its report in 2000, which also devoted systematic attention to the Canadian case.[24] The majority of its members sought to liberalize the Norwegian rules by allowing for dual citizenship and preventing the introduction of language requirements. However, in the end, the Citizenship Act, which was eventually adopted in 2006, rejected dual citizenship and introduced language requirements. Citizenship ceremonies were also introduced as part of the same policy process, although the ceremonies were not mentioned in the Citizenship Act.[25]

The introduction of language requirements and, especially, the citizenship ceremony were clearly inspired by Canadian practices. A key source claimed that there was a very strong link between the minister's study trip to Canada, where she attended a citizenship ceremony, and the formal introduction of citizenship ceremonies in Norway in 2007.[26] Apparently the entire delegation was impressed and seemed to think it was a good idea to celebrate the event of naturalization with a special ceremony, as is the case in Canada. Although in Norway the ceremonies are voluntary and have no legal function, those who elect to participate must take an oath of allegiance. The wording of the Norwegian and Canadian oaths are quite similar, which again points to the Canadian inspiration. The Norwegian oath reads as follows: "As a Norwegian national, I pledge loyalty to my country Norway and to Norwegian society, I support democracy and human rights and I will respect the laws of the country." The Canadian oath, which also includes a reference to Canada's constitutional monarch, is as follows: "I swear (or affirm) that I will be faithful and bear true allegiance to Her Majesty Queen Elizabeth the Second Queen of Canada, Her Heirs and Successors and that I will faithfully observe the laws of Canada and fulfil my duties as a Canadian citizen."

Although both Denmark and Sweden have introduced citizenship ceremonies, only the Norwegian one includes an oath of allegiance.[27] However, the Norwegian decision not to accept dual citizenship deviates from the Canadian approach to multiculturalism. As Brochmann and Hagelund note, both the White Paper on Diversity and the Citizenship Act demonstrate an ambivalence between efforts to strengthen the interests of the nation state and the community while also supporting the idea of individuals being more important than cultures regarding the rights of newcomers.[28] This ambivalence is reflected in the citizenship ceremony being voluntary rather than compulsory. The Introductory Act also established a stronger link between immigration control and integration policy by making the completion of a 300-hour course in the Norwegian language and knowledge of Norwegian society obligatory for both family and labour immigrants to obtain permanent residency and subsequent citizenship.[29]

In terms of integration policy, relatively generous economic resources are allocated to integration efforts in Norway, and the introduction programs provide for favourable learning conditions. Despite the rejection of dual citizenship, a central measure of the international Multiculturalism Policy Index, Norwegian multiculturalism policies were strengthened between 2000 and 2010 with an increase from 0 to 2.5 out of 8.[30] However, there is also much diversity since local municipalities have considerable freedom in controlling the use of their transferred funds for integration purposes.

Although family immigration still constitutes the largest group of immigrants entering Norway, labour immigration has received increased attention during the last decade.[31] Although regulated by the Immigration Act, the issue was considered by the Norwegian government in a white paper in 2008.[32] The Canadian model received special attention in the report itself, and Canada also played an important role in the preparatory work. In January 2007, the Norwegian minister for labour and social affairs, Bjarne Håkon Hanssen, led a delegation to Canada to learn about its approach to labour immigration. Upon his return, Hanssen praised the Canadian model.[33] Despite changes made over the years, Norwegian policies and practices in this area have not yet been comprehensively reformed. However, the Canadian model is still used as a reference in discussions on labour immigration, as demonstrated in the parliamentary debates over the most recent white paper on a comprehensive integration policy.[34]

Although the central administration of immigration and integration issues has been subject to a number of reorganizations during the past two decades,[35] Norwegian policies have not been reformed to the same extent as Danish and Swedish policies. Nevertheless, the Canadian model has received systematic attention in Norway since 2000 for a number of different reasons. First, Canada is often used as an example of a "traditional immigrant country" in contrast to a non-traditional immigration nation, such as Norway. The Immigration Law Committee consistently refers to Canada in these terms.[36] Thus inspiration and policy transfer can occur even when the actors involved recognize that the deeper domestic and immigration contexts differ.

Second, Canada's open and accommodating approach to immigration and increasing ethnic diversity, combined with its comprehensive welfare system, has also been used to justify the substantial attention devoted to the Canadian model. Representatives from the Welfare and Migration Committee highlighted this combination and referred to Canada as an "interesting contrast case" to Norway because Canadian and Norwegian immigration policies differ substantially while the two countries share a strong commitment to the welfare state.[37] These contextual differences and similarities are not only recognized, but may also be used actively in the policy transfer process.

Third, the Inclusion Committee is explicit in its justification: "Canada was selected because it was the first country in the world that in 1971 adopted an official multiculturalism policy."[38] Although national models are not static, the continued reference to the birth period or early formation of the Canadian immigration and integration policy model is revealing because it demonstrates the "stickiness" of national models in policy transfer and learning processes across countries. The early positive reputation of the Canadian model has been institutionalized and endures as a reference point for Norway. Although changes and fluctuations in the Canadian model may challenge this reputation, perceptions of a given national policy model are slow to change and unlikely to perfectly match the reality. Political processes are instead characterized by inefficient histories and lags in matching.[39]

Fourth, several of the interviewees confirmed that the Norwegian debate on multiculturalism was greatly shaped by the Canadian philosopher Will Kymlicka's writings on multiculturalism in liberal states, which are informed by Canadian experiences.[40] Through his influential publications and presentations to policy-makers in national and international forums, Kymlicka has – deliberately or not – significantly contributed to the genesis and diffusion of the Canadian model. In this respect, Duyvendak and Scholten's discussions of the "coproduction" of national models by academic researchers and policy-makers seem pertinent.[41]

Fifth, the Canadian model is also often used as a reference because it is a well-known and admired model. Canada is generally perceived as an international success in the area of immigration and integration policies. Several members of the three expert committees claimed that the Norwegian media often disseminated this message. A few selected headlines from Norwegian newspapers illustrate this point: "Look to Canada!,"[42] "Canadian model gives better integration,"[43] and "A multicultural society: The Norwegian political elite should look to Canada."[44] In an article entitled "Norwegian foolishness about integration," the author states that Norway should change course and instead "learn from Canada."[45] In these opinion pieces, the Canadian immigration and integration policy model is used as an image of success, a mythical model, without substantial background analysis. The media references therefore stand in deep contrast to the more systematic and scientific approach to the Canadian model taken by the Norwegian expert commissions. Nonetheless, the Canadian immigration and integration model continues to play a key role in the Norwegian media debate. For instance, a series of new references to Canada figured prominently in the Norwegian media after newly elected Prime Minister Trudeau made a commitment to receive 25,000 Syrian refugees – some of whom were welcomed by Trudeau himself at the airport – during the autumn of 2015. One such message was, "Look to Canada: Trudeau gives hope for progressive forces."[46]

Although both Canada's open and expansive policy on immigration control and its inclusive multiculturalist approach to immigrant integration have served as inspiration in the Norwegian reform debate and process between 2000 and 2015, the Canadian model has not always been viewed positively. For instance, a central member of the Inclusion Committee was highly critical of Canada's Temporary Foreign Worker Program, depicting it as a "calculated cynical immigration policy."[47] This critique effectively illustrates that would-be emulators, despite an overall positive image, also notice inconsistencies and incoherencies in the Canadian model. The practices and policies on temporary foreign workers were for instance regarded as being in opposition to Canada's inclusive multiculturalist approach to immigrant integration. As will be discussed in the concluding chapter of this book, the issue of temporary foreign workers may challenge the international reputation of the Canadian immigration and integration model in the long run.

Several interviewees also questioned the wisdom of evoking the Canadian model in the Norwegian context. Although learning from foreign models was seen as possible, several senior civil servants and members of expert committees voiced the need to adapt foreign models to Norwegian institutional and cultural frameworks. In general, the use of temporary expert committees in pre-legislative consultation processes has encouraged a more realistic and pragmatic perspective on the role of foreign national models in policy transfer and learning processes across countries. Several members of the expert committees argued that media and politicians often draw attention to specific elements of foreign models without considering them in a Norwegian context.[48]

Still Reassessing

The 2015 refugee crisis intensified the Norwegian debate on immigration and integration policy reforms. In late 2015, the minister of migration and integration of the conservative/right-wing minority coalition government, Sylvi Listhaug, presented a 150-page-long document containing forty concrete proposals for new asylum and migration regulations that she claimed would make Norway's policy "one of the strictest in Europe."[49] Listhaug represents the populist immigration-sceptic Progress Party, and the proposals included, among others:

- tighter restrictions on the right to family reunification;
- new and stricter integration criteria for permanent residence;
- greater opportunity to return people whose applications for asylum proved to be unfounded;
- reduced deadlines for lodging an appeal following the rejection of an application for asylum deemed to be unfounded;
- more effective ID clarification procedures;
- simplified processing routines for the refusal of applications;
- introduction of new categories of temporary protection, and a new category of protection that differentiates between refugees as defined in the UN Convention and others who cannot be returned to their country of origin due to other obligations under international law;
- introduction of temporary protection until the age of eighteen for unaccompanied minors; and
- a new legal basis for deciding not to consider individual applications from asylum seekers who enter Norway directly from a neighbouring Nordic country.[50]

The proposals generated much political debate, and more than 200 written comments from interested parties – ranging from political parties, non-governmental and governmental organizations, universities, to private individuals – were received by the six-week-long deadline for feedback. In the end, the government failed in June 2016 to summon the necessary parliamentary support for many of the most drastic reform proposals. For instance, the government failed to secure majority support to significantly tighten the rules for family reunification, which included specific demands for income and required those already in Norway to have studied or held a job in Norway for at least three years. Parliament also rejected the government's proposals to extend the residency requirements for immigrants from three to five years to obtain permanent residency, and to confine unaccompanied minors to temporary protection until they reach the legal age of eighteen. In her response to Parliament's rejection of these proposals for a stricter migration policy, Minister Listhaug stated, "This is primarily a shame for the Norwegian nation. We need a sustainable policy that safeguards the Norwegian welfare model. The level of immigration to Norway will be a decisive factor in this."[51] A few days after her disappointing outcome in Parliament, Minister Listhaug travelled to Canada. With direct relevance to the future sustainability of the Norwegian welfare model, the main purpose of this trip was to learn more about the Canadian private sponsorship program for refugees.[52]

Although the 2015 refugee crisis increased both the pace and the scope of the reform process in Norway, Norwegian immigration and integration policies were not reformed to the same extent as Danish and Swedish policies during the 2000–15 period. Instead, the process in Norway has been more incremental. A factor that may explain the slower pace in the Norwegian case is that there is less pressure to reform due to the absence of a general performance crisis. First, Norway has been more successful than the two other Scandinavian countries in integrating immigrants into the labour market. Although unemployment rates are significantly higher for foreign-born men and women than for native-born persons in Norway, the immigrant-native employment gap is larger in Denmark and Sweden (see Table 1 in chapter 1).[53] Second, the higher employment rates for both natives and immigrants are related to Norway's massive oil resources. According to Johan P. Olsen, oil money has in fact prevented the huge deficits that propelled public sector reforms in many other countries.[54] Thus, the Norwegian welfare state may be perceived as less vulnerable to problems stemming from increased immigration and lack of integration, at least in the short term.

As a result of both factors, comprehensive and immediate reforms have attracted less attention and support among politicians.

The potential benefits of incremental reforms may also explain Norway's status as a slow learner and reluctant reformer. The Norwegian state has historically been seen as a legitimate problem-solver where performance improvements are continuously sought through incremental changes.[55] Immigration and integration policy is no exception. Being a reluctant reformer, Norway has had the luxury of being able to evaluate the results of the more eager reformers like Denmark and Sweden, as well as the results of other models in the world. In this way, Norway has avoided "misspecified medicine" taken by others.[56]

Norway is still in the midst of the reassessment phase, and the Canadian immigration and integration policy model continues to be a central reference and an inspirational resource. In September 2014, fifteen members of the Parliamentary Standing Committee on Local Government and Public Administration spent almost a week in Canada to learn about immigrant integration efforts and the rights of Indigenous Peoples. According to one participant, a former government minister, Canada was chosen because Canada is viewed as a "pioneer" when it comes to dealing with these issues.[57] The Norwegian delegation visited representatives from a number of institutions in Quebec City and Toronto, including provincial and federal ministries of citizenship and immigration. A participant formulated the key impressions from the trip as follows: "The striking thing for me was that Canadian authorities so clearly state that they are happy about immigration and that they depend upon it, and that they say that multiculturalism is not a problem but a gift. This was emphasized everywhere … This is indeed very inspiring."[58]

In late 2015, the Norwegian government established a new expert committee, the Committee on the Long-Term Consequences of High Immigration (Utvalg om langsiktige konsekvenser av høy innvandring), to improve the knowledge base for policy decisions and to outline alternative strategies to meet challenges linked to continuing high levels of immigration. In order to achieve this, the committee was mandated to

- consider the extent to which continuing high immigration may affect social cohesion and trust in Norway;
- cast light on the socioeconomic consequences of high immigration and a growing proportion of the population having an immigrant background;

- consider how the Norwegian economy ought to adapt to continued high rates of immigration, particularly of refugees; and
- analyse the relationship between welfare schemes and immigration in Norway.

The committee was also asked to incorporate "knowledge and experience from comparable countries" into its analysis.[59] The role of and inspiration from the Canadian immigration and integration policy model in the work of this committee, which submitted its report on 1 February 2017, has yet to be determined. One thing is certain: Canada has a wealth of experience in carefully managing high levels of immigration, a fact that has already received much attention in Norway.

Whether Norway's slow learning and "reluctant reformer" approach to immigration and integration policy can be likened to Aesop's successful tortoise, slow and steady, or whether the tortoise will be too slow, remains to be seen.

PART THREE

Discussion and Conclusions

Chapter Five

Scandinavian Lesson-Drawing from Canada as "Work"

The choice of going to Canada [on a study trip] *was supported by all-party agreement ... The fact that Canada is a role model is acknowledged by the entire committee regardless of the political priorities the various parties have.*

Member of Parliament, Norway[1]

Thomas J. Anton's description of Swedish political culture from the 1960s became an influential and enduring portrayal that has been employed to study and understand Scandinavian policy-making generally.[2] "Extraordinarily deliberative," "highly rationalistic," "very open," and "consensual" – these were the key properties, Anton argued, that created a distinct "politics as work" rather than a "politics as game" orientation to policy-making. According to Anton, Swedish style policy-making and political culture seemed to be "almost totally devoid of ideological or philosophical symbolism, focusing instead on specific proposals to deal with specific problems."[3]

Contrary to Anton's account, policy transfer and lesson-drawing from abroad have in general been described as highly contested endeavours where political adversaries use foreign lessons selectively and strategically as weapons in domestic debates.[4] Information about the effects of programs elsewhere may serve the purpose of justifying prior positions,[5] or policy lessons from other polities may be used to "manipulate contested ideas" in order to "bias the outcome of the policy-making process."[6] When proponents of a specific policy program portray a similar program in another polity in overly positive terms (while opponents of the same program exaggerate the negatives), lesson-drawing takes on a clear "politics as game" orientation, to use Anton's terminology. However, Anton's depictions of Swedish policy-making as "work" can be recognized in the way Denmark, Norway, and Sweden draw policy lessons from abroad today. Scandinavian lesson-drawing from Canada in the highly politicized field of immigration and integration policies is largely deliberative, rationalistic, open, and consensual.

Although policy transfer research has recently been depicted as a "growth industry,"[7] the wider contextual factors of these processes have received little attention. Bulmer and Padgett provide a useful starting point for addressing this deficiency.[8] In their study of the European Union, they demonstrate that transfer processes and outcomes are shaped by the institutional settings and governance regimes in which they take place. In particular, stronger forms of policy transfer seem to occur in more highly institutionalized governance regimes. This chapter demonstrates the strong link between Scandinavian-style policy-making and lesson-drawing from abroad.

Lesson-Drawing as "Work" versus "Game"

Lesson-drawing and policy transfer both refer to processes by which knowledge of policies, administrative arrangements, institutions, and ideas in one political setting (past or present) are used in the development of policies, administrative arrangements, institutions, and ideas in another political system.[9] However, distinctions between the two concepts are also made. While policy transfer tends to cover both the "voluntary" and more "coercive" aspects of these processes, lesson-drawing focuses on the "voluntary" transfer that occurs as a result of the free choices of political actors.[10]

Voluntary transfer is driven by some form of dissatisfaction with the status quo, and according to Rose, "the process of lesson-drawing starts with scanning programmes in effect elsewhere, and ends with the prospective evaluation of what would happen if a programme already in effect elsewhere were transferred here in future."[11] This definition encompasses several steps and activities. Focus in this chapter is on the processes through which information from abroad is gathered, analysed, and evaluated; the participants involved, their agendas and strategies, and the level of conflict among them – all considered to be central policy-style characteristics.[12]

Anton's depiction of Swedish policy-making as extraordinarily deliberative, highly rationalistic, very open, and consensual was said to characterize a distinctive "politics as work" rather than a "politics as game" orientation to policy-making.[13] Although there are clear overlaps among Anton's properties, he claimed that Swedish policy-making was *deliberative* in the sense that it took long periods of time during which well-trained specialists gave more or less constant attention to a given problem. He identified formally appointed expert commissions of inquiry as principal sites for extended deliberations on policy alternatives. In addition to internal deliberations, the commissions sought external feedback from stakeholders and interested parties. According to Anton, the feedback was actually taken seriously.

Policy-making was also *rationalistic* in that great efforts were made to acquire the most information possible about any given issue, including thorough reviews of historical experiences and a wide range of alternatives proffered by Swedish as well as foreign scholars. The gathered information was then approached and analysed in what Anton referred to as a "highly pragmatic intellectual style."[14] Anton's interpretations of Swedish policy-making did not assume perfect rationality. However, he drew attention to a particular system of policy-making where problem-solving was greatly valued.[15] Related to Anton's notion of "rationality," "scientific policy-making" is another phrase that has been used to describe the Scandinavian approach,[16] while Lundqvist and Petersen talk about the "alliance of science and policy."[17]

In addition, Anton claimed that Swedish policy-making was *open* in the sense that completed expert reports were submitted to an appropriate ministry, which immediately circulated copies to all interested parties and organizations inviting consultations prior to final decision-making. Based on the extensive use of hearings, Goodin would later agree with Anton, referring to the Scandinavian countries as "consultative polities."[18]

Furthermore, Anton characterized Swedish policy-making as *consensual* in that decisions were seldom made without the agreement of virtually all parties. The consensus mode of policy-making in Scandinavia has often been contrasted with the more confrontational majoritarian style of the Anglo-American world.[19] Policy-making in Scandinavia proceeds in accordance with a "sounding out" process, rather than with majorities pressing things to a vote as quickly as possible.[20] According to Anton, the desire for consensus sometimes means that controversial issues take a long time to resolve. As a result, decision-making "never seems rash, abrupt, irrational, or indeed, exciting."[21]

Although what has been referred to as the "Anton model" was originally developed almost fifty years ago, central properties of the model were later reconfirmed by Anton,[22] and they are also recognized in

Scandinavian policy-making today.[23] Importantly, the Anton model is manifest in Scandinavian lesson-drawing from Canada in the areas of immigration and integration policy between 2000 and 2015.

Drawing Lessons from the Canadian Immigration and Integration Policy Model in Denmark, Norway, and Sweden

Scandinavian Lesson-Drawing as Deliberative:
The Role of Expert Commissions

Formally appointed expert commissions of inquiry played a central role in the reassessment of Scandinavian immigration and integration policies. Although the size, composition, duration, and mandates varied, analyses of international experiences constituted an important background for the commissions' deliberations on policy alternatives. Several of these committees engaged directly in lesson-drawing from the Canadian immigration and integration policy model.

In Denmark, both the Think Tank on Integration (Tænketanken om utfordinger for integrationsindsatsen i Danmark) and the Welfare Commission (Velfærdskommissionen) emphasized the importance of analysing international experiences in immigration and integration policy, and Canada received substantial attention by both expert commissions.[24] In Norway, the Welfare and Migration Committee (Velferds- og migrasjonsutvalget) was established to assess the impact of increased migration on the Norwegian welfare system. It was mandated to "have a comparative perspective, where developments in other Nordic countries and other countries must be assessed and compared to relevant trends in Norway."[25] The Inclusion Committee (Inkluderingsutvalget), which evaluated challenges and made proposals for a multicultural Norway, also devoted special attention to integration efforts in Canada, Denmark, France, Germany, Sweden, and the United Kingdom.[26]

Three central Swedish committees also made many references to the Canadian model: the Citizenship Committee (1997 års medborgarskapskommitté) was created to revise existing laws on citizenship; the Family Immigration Committee (Anhörigkommittén) was initiated to evaluate the rules on family reunification; and the Labour Immigration Committee (Kommittén för arbetskraftsinvandring) was established to assess Swedish legislation on labour immigration.

The deliberations in these committees were often intense. According to a central member of the Norwegian Immigration Law Committee

(Utlendingslovsutvalget), members disagreed about specific issues.[27] Despite lengthy discussions, for example, the committee did not reach agreement on the length of time an immigrant would be required to live in Norway to obtain permanent residency. While a minority of the members preferred five years, the majority argued for maintaining the three-year requirement.[28] As a background for their deliberations, the various inquiry commissions actively considered foreign policy experiences, including the Canadian immigration and integration model, in a rationalistic, and even scientific, manner.

*Scandinavian Lesson-Drawing as Rationalistic:
Scientific Problem-Solving*

In all commissions mentioned, expertise outside of government played a key role in the policy deliberations. The five-member Danish Think Tank on Integration included two university professors and three civil servants. The Welfare Commission was appointed by the Liberal/Conservative government to address the future challenges to the Danish welfare state system. It was comprised of nine members, including four academic researchers, three representatives from the private business sector, and two representatives from non-governmental organizations. The two Norwegian commissions were diverse in terms of membership and derived expertise from current and former civil servants, representatives from the academic sector, and organized interests. The size of the Norwegian committees varied from eight (Welfare and Migration Committee) to seventeen members (Inclusion Committee). The Swedish commissions consisted of members of Parliament from the various political parties with support from civil service experts. The size of the committees varied from ten to more than twenty members. The convention in Denmark and Norway is to make appointees who are not parliamentarians. Only Sweden maintains the practice of including parliamentarians on inquiry commissions.[29]

As a background for their deliberations, the various committees systematically gathered information about foreign models, including the Canadian model. Several civil servants emphasized how new technologies had facilitated information gathering, with integration and immigration regulations and laws now readily available through internet.[30] The commissions also contacted foreign authorities for information. For instance, the Swedish Labour Immigration Committee distributed questionnaires about labour immigration conditions to a number of countries through Swedish embassies.[31] Several committee members also mentioned possibilities for study trips abroad if more information should be needed. It is quite common for Scandinavian commissions to embark on such study trips. Both the Norwegian Immigration Law Committee (Utlendingslovsutvalget) and the Welfare and Migration Committee went on study trips to several countries.[32]

In addition to relying on its own expert counsel, commissions sought external advice. The Norwegian Welfare and Migration Committee commissioned the expertise of Canadian academic, Keith Banting, to write a report on the Canadian model, incorporated into its final report in 2011.[33] The committee engaged Banting because its members wanted to rely directly on Canadian expertise rather than solely on their own impressions and analyses of the Canadian model.[34]

As grist for its deliberations, the Family Immigration Committee in Sweden also relied on information provided by the immigration authorities in Canada. Moreover, the committee secretariat visited the Canadian embassy in Stockholm to supplement its knowledge of the Canadian family integration system.[35] External expertise likewise played a role in Denmark, where a comprehensive background study, produced by the Danish National Centre for Social Research (SFI), formed a referential backdrop for the deliberations of the Think Tank on Integration.[36] In addition to the commissions' internal deliberations, draft commission proposals were widely distributed to interested parties for feedback, demonstrating the openness of Scandinavian lesson-drawing.

Scandinavian Lesson-Drawing as Open: Institutionalized Consultations

Recommendations of ad hoc expert inquiry commissions are generally widely circulated for the purposes of consultation and external deliberation. In Norway and Sweden, recommendations are published in the respective government's official report series, the NOUs (Norges offentlige utredninger) and the SOUs (Statens offentliga utredningar). All interested parties, including public authorities, non-governmental organizations (NGOs), and even private individuals, may provide input on the recommendations presented by the ad hoc inquiry commissions before final political decisions are made. Normally, a three-month deadline for feedback is given.

Although the consultation system is more formalized in Norway and Sweden compared with Denmark,[37] both the Danish Think Tank on Integration and the Welfare Commission widely circulated their reports. From a perspective of lesson-drawing from abroad, both Danish commissions prepared special comparative reports about the situation in other countries.[38]

Invitations for consultation normally generate considerable feedback. For instance, the report from the Norwegian Welfare and Migration Committee, which was delivered in May 2011, received written comments from fifty-two different interested parties in a short period.[39] In the same year, the Inclusion Committee's report received seventy-three written comments in an equally short period.[40] Advice from consultations often leads to policy changes. For example, the Ministry of Regional Affairs in Norway originally recommended citizenship ceremonies without an oath of allegiance, but changed its mind in response to input from the hearings held in 2003.[41] Feedback from the Resource Centre for Pakistani Children was quoted at length and seemed, in particular, to justify the change of mind: "In a society marked by ever increasing ethnic diversity, we view it as important to set conditions for Norwegian citizenship. The transition to Norwegian citizenship should include an emphasis and celebration of the fundamental values of society. In order to ensure the society's message, new citizens should declare an oath of allegiance in a solemn ceremony."[42]

Although responses from consulted parties are usually varied, the consultation process has consequences for the level of conflict in policy-making. The fact that opposition and policy alternatives can be expressed through institutionalized structures and processes does not eliminate conflict, but it tends to "domesticate" it by reducing the possibility of public conflict.[43] By providing opportunities for participation, consultations and hearings provide input legitimacy to Scandinavian policy-making and lesson-drawing.

Scandinavian Lesson-Drawing as Consensual: Pragmatic Adaptation

Scandinavian lesson-drawing as consensual comprises several dimensions. First, there is a broad consensus among Scandinavian policy actors, from civil servants to politicians, that lessons can actually be drawn from abroad. Second, there is an overwhelming consensus that lesson-drawing requires systematic analyses of foreign policies and programs over time. Third, consensus is apparent apropos the results of the lesson-drawing exercise. All policy-making participants and practitioners emphasized that foreign policies and programs must be modified and adjusted to adapt to domestic circumstances.

Due to the consensus on motivations for and methods of lesson-drawing from abroad, spending public money on foreign study trips is not a very controversial topic in Scandinavia. Members of Parliament in the Scandinavian countries have been allocated generous travel budgets, and parliamentary committees embark regularly on both European and overseas study trips. In the Swedish case, parliamentary committees had a total budget of 20,5 million kroner (approximately $3,1 million CDN) for foreign travels for the 2010–14 period.[44] It is true that Scandinavian media sometimes questions the value-added of expensive foreign study trips,[45] but the civil servants and politicians interviewed for this study seemed to agree on their usefulness. In particular, the study trips were seen as a source of inspiration for the development of new ideas. Time and costs involved are thought to be reasonable, but in any event, both are transparent for public scrutiny. For instance, the Norwegian Parliament posts on its website all scheduled study trips and committee travels well in advance.[46] The same information is available on the websites of the Danish and Swedish Parliaments.[47]

Among Scandinavian politicians and civil servants, there is also consensus about the relevance of Canada as a potential model for immigration and integration. A Norwegian MP and former cabinet minister, a participant on a study trip to Canada in 2014, expressed a widespread sentiment of its value: "The choice of going to Canada was supported by all-party agreement … The fact that Canada is a role model is acknowledged by the entire committee regardless of the political priorities the various parties have."[48]

In addition to the motivations for and methods of lesson-drawing from abroad, there is widespread agreement that foreign solutions will not always be desirable or practical in Scandinavia. Therefore, the Canadian model was not entirely copied or emulated. Instead, it has served as an intellectual stimulus and a model of inspiration. As demonstrated, Canadian inspiration has significantly shaped Scandinavian immigration and integration reform debates and processes between 2000 and 2015.

Practical Lesson-Drawing

Motivations for and methods of policy transfer and lesson-drawing from abroad have received scant attention in the growing literature. Dolowitz and Marsh comment only briefly on the distinction between "practical" and "ideological" motivations for engaging in such processes.[49]

Using Anton's distinction between politics as "work" as opposed to a "game," this present study illustrates that Scandinavian lesson-drawing from Canada between 2000 and 2015 on immigration and integration policy was highly practical and "work-oriented." Thus Scandinavian policy-making and lesson-drawing styles are closely linked: both can be characterized as extraordinarily deliberative, highly rationalistic, very open, and consensual.

Canada as an Inspirational, but Not Always Practical or Desirable Model: The Politics of Pragmatism

Essentially united as one family, yes, but with strong intra-family differences too. Unity is prized, but each member-nationality in the family group has an individuality to maintain even while cooperating with the group. Hence each people and country must be considered independently.

Franklin D. Scott[1]

Danish, Norwegian, and Swedish approaches to immigration control and immigrant integration are marked by both similarities and differences. Denmark, Norway, and Sweden have recently received a near record number of immigrants, representing more than 1 per cent of the population annually. Immigrants joining their families, and refugees, constitute the largest groups in all three countries. However, Denmark's assimilationist approach to immigrant integration stands in deep contrast to Sweden's multiculturalist approach. The country case studies demonstrate that Sweden over time has moved closer to the Canadian model. By 2015, Sweden was characterized by inclusive multiculturalism and open and expansive immigration policies (Figure 6). Despite an increased focus and openness towards labour immigration, Denmark is placed in the exclusionist and restrictive/culturally assimilationist segment of the figure. Danish family reunification policies are, for instance, among the most restrictive in the world. Norway is positioned somewhere between Denmark and Sweden on both dimensions. Although Norway has moved closer to Denmark in terms of both immigration control and immigrant integration during the past decade, Norway displays more aspects of multicultural policies than Denmark (for instance, more funding of ethnic group organizations and activities, bilingual education, and mother tongue instruction), according to the Multiculturalism Policy Index.[2]

Figure 6. Immigration and integration policies in Canada, Denmark, Norway, and Sweden in 2015

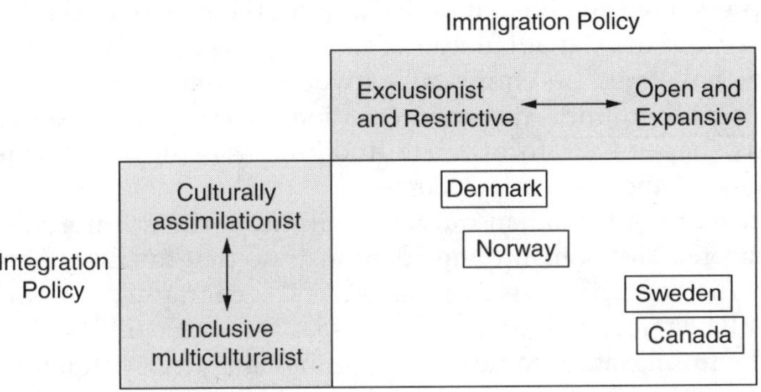

Despite the growing transatlantic convergence between Canada and Sweden, there is still a fundamental difference between the two countries: The deeply entwined relationship between immigration control and immigrant integration, the defining characteristic of the Canadian model, is not evident in Sweden. Although both Canada and Sweden are characterized by open and expansive immigration policies (about 20 per cent of Canada's population and 17 per cent of Sweden's population are born outside the country), the composition of the immigrant population in the two countries differs significantly. While economic immigrants constitute the largest category in Canada, refugees and their families is the largest in Sweden. Because economic immigrants, in general, perform better in the labour market than refugees,[3] employment rates for immigrants are significantly higher in Canada than in Sweden.[4] Economic immigration has therefore often been said to differ from refugee flows and family reunification movements in that the immigrants involved are "wanted"; that is, they are accepted not out of some obligation to humanitarian ideals or international law, but rather out of self-interests.[5] Canada's geographic isolation from global conflicts and from extreme poverty has undoubtedly facilitated the focus on economic immigrants. However, the immigration strategy is carefully managed to promote integration. This is a key reason why the Canadian immigration and integration policy model is considered to be so successful.

Canada as an International Model

Previous chapters have demonstrated that although the distinctiveness and cohesiveness of the Canadian immigration and integration policy model can be challenged on empirical, as well as on epistemological and methodological grounds, it is an internationally recognized model that has greatly shaped the reform debate and process in the three Scandinavian countries since the early 2000s.

The relevance of the Canadian model for Scandinavia is intriguing for several reasons: First, our findings demonstrate that the Canadian model, a product of unique sociopolitical and geographic circumstances, can still be relevant to other countries lacking these underlying conditions. The immigration context in Scandinavia is clearly different from that in Canada. Thus, the Canadian model is relevant for other countries lacking similar underlying conditions, despite claims to the contrary.[6] Second, the Canadian model's status as an international model in Scandinavia demonstrates that a country typically described in the public policy literature as a "policy borrower" can act as a model and "policy lender" for countries that have customarily served as policy lenders or exporters. This assertion, of course, challenges much of the established literature on the relationship between policy lenders and borrowers.[7] Third, the fact that Canadian immigration and integration policies are well known in Scandinavia suggests that the active promotion of the Canadian model by successive Canadian governments has succeeded. Several of the Canadian and Scandinavian politicians, civil servants, and policy experts interviewed suggested as much. This study therefore demonstrates that Canada's international leadership role in immigration and integration policy serves as an effective way of promoting Canada internationally, a key goal of Canada's foreign policy. Fourth, the Scandinavian attraction to the Canadian model between 2000 and 2015 has endured despite several changes of government in both Canada and in the three Scandinavian countries. The relevance of the Canadian model to Scandinavia is not founded on closely matching political ideologies of governing parties. The positive reputation of the Canadian immigration and integration model has to a large extent been institutionalized in Scandinavia, which illustrates the "stickiness" of national models in policy transfer and learning processes across countries. A national model's credibility internationally does not change immediately with changes in domestic policies and practices. Therefore, there is unlikely to be a perfect match between the existence of a given national policy model and the perception of this model internationally. Policy transfer processes are instead characterized by inefficient histories and lags in matching.[8]

Policy Transfer from Canada to Scandinavia

Driven by dissatisfaction with the status quo, the Scandinavian countries have engaged extensively in voluntary policy transfer from Canada. Policy transfer has mainly been of the soft type, that is, the transfer of ideas, concepts, and attitudes.[9] In particular, the Canadian immigration and integration policy model has served as an inspirational model and has been used as an intellectual stimulus for new policies and programs in Scandinavia. Canada's positive view of immigrants as resources has inspired new attitudes towards labour immigration in Denmark, Norway, and Sweden during the 2000s. Canada's focus on skilled economic immigrants – a group that integrates more easily into the labour market – has received much attention as an alternative to the concentration on humanitarian and family migrants that has contributed to the immigrant-native employment gap in Scandinavia. However, the general notion of an increasingly open and selective immigration strategy has prompted different responses in the three countries that all differed from the original Canadian programs and policies.

With direct relevance to the future of the Scandinavian welfare states, the Canadian emphasis on immigrants' own responsibility for integrating into the labour market and society has resonated in Denmark, Norway, and Sweden. A greater emphasis on activation, the act of transferring responsibility to the service users for their active and productive role in society, has brought the Scandinavian countries closer to the Canadian model.[10] According to a recent statement by the Norwegian government, the state will in the future be far more involved with refugees and their families than with migrant workers from countries both within and outside the EEA and the EU. "Migrant workers must themselves arrange financial support and accommodation; in addition, they have to use ordinary services and do not qualify for the introduction programme for immigrants."[11]

Specific processes demonstrate the more active emulation of Canadian policies and programs (see Table 3). Norway's adoption of citizenship ceremonies and Denmark's use of the points system for economic immigrants were openly transferred from Canada. The Canadian model has also played a role in the process that led to the acceptance of

Table 3. Policy transfer from the Canadian immigration and integration policy model to Scandinavian countries

Type of transfer	Denmark	Norway	Sweden
Inspiration	The Canadian positive view of immigration and immigrants as a resource contributed to a rediscovery of labour immigration in all three Scandinavian countries.		
Emulation	"points system" for labour immigration	citizenship ceremonies	dual citizenship
Copying	n/a	n/a	n/a
Non-transfer	Several policies and programs were not transferred as they were deemed to be either politically undesirable or technically impractical in the Scandinavian context. For instance, Canadian programs for private sponsorship of refugees have so far been met with little enthusiasm in the state-oriented welfare regimes in Scandinavia.		

dual citizenship in Sweden. However, Canadian policies and programs in these areas were all modified and adjusted to domestic circumstances. Direct and complete transfer in terms of copying did not occur in the reform process. This implies that Scandinavian reformers did not perceive the Canadian immigration and integration policy model as a "ready-to-use exemplary model."[12] Fundamental differences between the Canadian and Scandinavian welfare state regimes can explain why soft policy transfer of ideas, concepts, and attitudes dominated. The fact that the comprehensive Scandinavian welfare state is characterized by universal coverage, whereas Canada's welfare state is more residual and focused on needs, discouraged direct and complete transfer.

Although the Norwegian citizenship ceremonies differ from the Canadian ones they emulated – voluntary instead of obligatory, for instance – the purpose is the same: to celebrate the event of becoming naturalized. The introduction of citizenship ceremonies in Norway has been a success with both the number of ceremonies and the participation rates increasing. According to a Norwegian study, the total participation rate was approximately 20 per cent of all invited in the first year, and those who participated tended to be "very happy about the experience."[13] Reasons for participating varied from a strong desire to communicate a sense of belonging to Norway to mere curiosity. Reasons for not participating included never having received an invitation, inconvenience, too busy, or simply a failure to see the point in attending.[14] Altogether twenty-six ceremonies were organized in Norway in 2015, and the participation rate varied between 35 per cent and 17 per cent in the various counties. The introduction of citizenship ceremonies in Norway therefore represents a lasting inspiration from the Canadian model.

Distinctive political-administrative histories, cultures, traditions, and styles of governance in the Scandinavian countries have also led to non-transfer of certain aspects of the Canadian immigration and integration policy model. In particular, Canadian programs for the private sponsorship of refugees have so far been met with little enthusiasm from the state-oriented welfare regimes in Scandinavia. A Norwegian high-ranking civil servant bluntly expressed his scepticism towards private sponsorship: "Privatization, like it is practiced in Canada, is a distant thought in the Scandinavian welfare states."[15] Likewise, the adoption of a Canadian-style points system was seen as contrary to Swedish cultural values. Similarly, Canadian-style multiculturalism has been rejected outright in Denmark. Canada's Temporary Foreign Worker Program has also been criticized in Scandinavia for being unfair.

According to Richard Rose, every policy or program can be appraised by two very different standards: "Is it practical? Is it desirable?"[16] Actors engaging in policy transfer processes must address both questions. While the articulation of desires is alleged to be the legitimate domain of elected officials, the determination of what is possible is a primary concern of career officials and experts.[17] The policy transfer between the Canadian immigration and integration policy model and the three Scandinavian countries confirms as much.

Based on perceptions of domestic policy failure, political competition, and public disquiet, elected officials in Scandinavia have been central actors in the process of seeking inspiration and learning from abroad. Several interviewees confirm that the Canadian model has attracted particular attention from politicians in Denmark, Norway, and Sweden because it was widely recognized as a successful solution, particularly by Scandinavian media. However, expert commissions, supported by professional secretariats, have played a crucial role in the reassessment of Danish, Norwegian, and Swedish immigration and integration policies, but more so in Norway and Sweden than in Denmark. Information about the Canadian model has been collected through different methods. Research was conducted on Canadian websites. Canadian experts and expertise were consulted from a distance but also through organized study trips to Canada. Data and references to the Canadian model were then supported by methodical discussions of the model's advantages and disadvantages in the Scandinavian context.

In line with this systematic approach, several bureaucrats and civil servants warned politicians against attempts at direct and complete (hard) policy transfer or copying of Canadian policies and programs. Politicians would often have to be reminded that a particular foreign policy solution had to fit with the domestic realities. Thus, according to a high-ranking civil servant, "This is the job of the civil servants in the ministries: saying 'no' to politicians. A particular measure may be a good idea, but it may not fit with our overall system. Instead, our job is to present ideas to the politicians that will fit with the government's overall policy line."[18] A member of a Norwegian expert inquiry commission claimed that politicians will often come to such realizations on their own: "I think well-informed, clever and honest politicians will discover that it is not acceptable to import solutions from other countries; it is just not realistic. However, politicians, as others, can be inspired by particular solutions."[19] Indeed, the central role of experts and civil servants ensured that the question of practicality was addressed in the Scandinavian policy transfer from the Canadian model.

Although the Canadian immigration and integration policy model was portrayed and promoted as a particularly successful, and almost mythical, model by politicians and media in Scandinavia, the way in which this model was used in Denmark, Norway, and Sweden since the turn of the century corresponds well with a structural-instrumental perspective. Systematic discussions of the Canadian model's advantages and disadvantages, based on means-ends rationality and cultural compatibility with the Scandinavian context, dominated the process. Information about the Canadian model was therefore not primarily used selectively and strategically as a weapon in domestic debates to justify prior positions or to manipulate contested ideas, as the policy transfer process has often been described in the literature.[20] Policy transfer processes in Scandinavia should be perceived as "work" rather than "game," which reconfirms the well-established view of Scandinavian countries as rationalistic or even scientific with respect to policy-making.[21]

In addition to policy transfer from the Canadian immigration and integration policy model to Scandinavia, Canada has in turn benefited from international exchanges on policy experiences. In particular, the special relationship between Canada and Sweden has demonstrated signs of mutual inspiration, which may result in the refinement and improvement of the Canadian model. For instance, Sweden's experiences in handling a high intake of refugees may yield lessons for

Canada. From a research perspective, this relationship confirms the value of adopting an extended time frame and viewing policy transfer and learning processes as iterative and reciprocal exchanges.[22] The special relationship that has developed between Canada and Sweden effectively demonstrates the Scandinavian variation in this policy transfer process.

Scandinavian Variation

Scandinavian politics is a history of similarities and differences among nations. In reference to the 1940s and 1950s, Marklund aptly summarizes Hinshaw and Scott's identification of a principal similarity that produces different outcomes, pragmatism: "Scandinavian 'pragmatism' was based on 'common ideology' as they paradoxically phrased it, which was united in its attempts to 'equalize opportunity for all people' and producing similar results across the whole region, although – in true pragmatic fashion – the solutions 'varied in detail in the different lands.'"[23]

Scandinavian pragmatism has been applied to the Canadian model in that it has not been accepted and transferred as a complete package of reforms. Instead, individual Scandinavian countries have considered only selected policy elements of the model. The Canadian model has been filtered, edited, and redefined in a process of practical or pragmatic adaptation.[24] There were significant differences among Denmark, Norway, and Sweden in this process. Although all three countries have viewed Canada as an inspirational model, a unique and particularly close policy relationship – based on regular and frequent contacts and interactions – has emerged between Sweden and Canada. The special relationship with Canada may be due to Sweden's longer experience with immigration than its two Scandinavian neighbours. Sweden signed its first state agreements for the recruitment of foreign labour with Austria, Hungary, and Italy as early as 1947, and by the 1950s Sweden was already pursuing a policy of actively promoting labour immigration both through organized recruitment schemes and via liberal immigration regulations.[25] Denmark and Norway started a decade later, and shortly after that, in the mid-1960s, demands for immigration restrictions surfaced in all three countries.

In addition, Sweden stands out from its Scandinavian counterparts due to its early adoption of a radical multicultural policy in 1975. Since then, immigrants have been treated on equal footing with national minorities.[26] Kymlicka has made the general argument that multiculturalism policies in Europe, unlike in Canada, were first introduced as part of a guest worker policy; that is, multicultural measures were introduced not to promote integration and citizenship but to make it easier for foreign workers and their children to return to their "home" countries when unneeded by the labour markets.[27] However, Borevi challenges Kymlicka's argument in the case of Sweden. She claims that the guest worker model was explicitly rejected at an early stage in Sweden as demonstrated by the introduction in 1954 of a "special residence permit" offering greater security to "foreigners who chose to settle permanently."[28] Furthermore, Borevi argues that multicultural ideas, which emerged in the mid-1960s, were explicitly linked to the overarching goal of promoting integration rather than facilitating the return of immigrants to their "home" countries.

Another reason for the close policy relationship between Canada and Sweden is that Sweden has far more immigrants than Denmark and Norway, both in absolute terms and as a proportion of the population. Sweden currently has about three times as many immigrants as Norway and Denmark – 1.7 million compared with 0.7 and 0.5 million, respectively. In 2015, 17 per cent of the Swedish population was foreign born. The equivalent share in Norway and Denmark was 13 and 10 per cent, respectively.[29] Swedish realities are therefore more similar to Canadian realities than Danish and Norwegian migration demographics.

The objective of ensuring the future of the welfare state may be another factor that explains divergent Scandinavian approaches. The Danish welfare state's relative generosity compared with Sweden's may go a long way in explaining Denmark's more restrictive approach to immigration control and immigrant integration.[30] Large revenues from the oil and gas sector have made Norway a unique case, and this economically solid position has created less pressure for welfare state reforms to reduce expenditure.[31] Norway's resource-rich economy may also explain its slower tempo in the immigration and integration policy reform process.

Yet another reason to explain the Swedish exceptionalism is that public attitudes towards immigration have been more positive in Sweden than in Denmark and Norway. According to the European Social Survey, Sweden is consistently cited as the most "immigrant friendly" country in Europe, well ahead of both Norway and Denmark.[32] By contrast, Danes and Norwegians are more suspicions than Swedes that immigrants may deliberately seek to cheat and take advantage of the generous welfare systems and decline to integrate into the larger society while dependent on public support. According to Yngve Lithman, these qualms are virtually absent from Swedish and Canadian discourse: "In both of these countries, the general tenor of discussion is that immigrants are anxious to establish themselves as independent people rather than wards of the state."[33] Recent research has documented that public support for welfare chauvinism or dualism, defined as the introduction of a two-tier welfare system where the access to benefits and/or the generosity of benefits is systematically differentiated between immigrants and the general population, is substantial in both Denmark and Norway.[34] Forty-seven per cent of Danes reported to agree completely or partly with the idea of withholding social assistance from immigrants, and 37 per cent of the Norwegian sample did the same.[35]

Furthermore, Sweden, like Canada and unlike Denmark and Norway, did not have a strong anti-immigration party during the first decade of the twenty-first century. The anti-immigrant Sweden Democrats (Sverigedemokraterna) won representation in Parliament for the first time in 2010. By contrast, the Danish People's Party (Dansk Folkeparti) wielded a strong influence on the Danish centre-right government from 2001 until 2011. Norway's middle road between the two is partly due to the limited, direct influence that the Progress Party (Fremskrittspartiet) has had on government policies, despite having the support of about 20 per cent of the electorate throughout the 2000s. This changed in 2013 when the party became a partner in a minority coalition government. Although the Progress Party has brought a tougher rhetoric on immigration control and immigrant integration to the government offices, the actual policies differ little from those of previous governments.

Although not always practical or desirable, the Canadian immigration and integration policy model has served as an instrumental, inspirational model in Denmark, Norway, and Sweden. Immigration and integration policy issues are still high on the political agenda, and the three Scandinavian countries continue to engage in foreign lesson-drawing and to look for inspiration abroad in their ongoing reassessments of policies and practices. It remains to be seen, however, whether the Canadian model will continue to serve as a source of inspiration.

A Note on the Future of the Canadian Model: Change and Continuity

National models, including the Canadian immigration and integration policy model, are not static. Nor are their international reputations, which may be affected by changes in policies and practices. For example, policy inconsistencies may challenge the attractiveness of the Canadian model internationally. It has been alleged that the Conservative government (2006 to 2015) weakened Canada's reputation among other countries due to its unfair treatment of temporary foreign workers.[36] The government dramatically increased the number of temporary foreign workers, and it was blamed for creating a system with "major protection gaps" between workers in workplace health and safety, employment standards, health care, and access to compensation.[37] Lenard and Straehle warned that "without immediate policy shifts, Canada risks jeopardizing what has otherwise been rightly interpreted as its just and fair immigration regime, which has, at least historically, been identified as a model to emulate."[38]

Another criticism has been the growing imbalance between the number of economic immigrants and refugees arriving in Canada. The 35,774 refugees that Canada received in 2005 dropped to 23,286 by 2014.[39] During the same period, the number of economic immigrants grew significantly. Canada receives among the highest numbers per capita of new immigrants in the world, but is ranked much lower in accepting refugees per capita.[40] The growing imbalance between economic immigrants and refugees was debated during the 2015 general election campaign and at the height of the Syrian refugee crisis.[41] Critics argue that a country that is actively recruiting immigrants as economic assets has a special obligation to also receive substantial numbers of those fleeing persecution and oppression.[42]

Indeed, Naurin and Öhberg, claiming that a fundamental transformation has recently occurred in the Swedish discourse concerning the Canadian model, argue that Canada's reputation has already been damaged: "Some years ago, political parties in Sweden saw Canada's immigration program as exemplary. They sent delegations to Canada to learn about its successful integration of immigrants. However, these delegations stopped crossing the Atlantic when they learned more about differences between how the two countries perceive immigration. Instead of being a model, Canada is now treated as an example of a self-centered and unfair immigration system."[43] However, Naurin and Öhberg's comments are not congruent with our data on Swedish visits to Canada and with opinions drawn from our interviews with Swedish and Scandinavian civil servants and politicians. The Canadian immigration and integration policy model still serves as an inspirational model for Sweden and the two other Scandinavian countries.

Systematic analyses of the international relevance of the Canadian model over time have not been conducted. However, the reputation of the model will depend upon whether it can be pragmatically adapted to changing circumstances while at the same time staying true to its defining characteristics. A fundamental aspect of the Canadian model is that *both* Canada as a country and immigrants themselves seem to have benefited from immigration. Both sides should be considered when addressing the future of the Canadian immigration and integration policy model as an international model. Thus, according to Reitz, "Canada's attempts to reinvent its own policy model in response to current problems are aided by the country's strong and continuing commitment to immigration and its positive opportunities."[44] In this context, the dynamic relationship between public opinion on the one hand, and elite politics and actual immigration and integration policies on the other, must be carefully monitored. In Canada, government has traditionally had the confidence of the public to manage migration to the benefit of Canadians. The future of the Canadian model and its international reputation depend upon whether it can be pragmatically adapted to maintain this bargain.

Recent changes in Canadian immigration and integration policies and practices reflect different trends. While reforms have been introduced that represent a pragmatic adaptation of the Canadian model to changing circumstances – adaptations that may maintain and even enhance Canada's international reputation – other reforms are more problematic for the long-term survival of the Canadian model as an admired model internationally.

Increased efforts to strengthen Canadian citizenship and more focus and reliance on economic immigrants can be seen as pragmatic adaptations to new challenges. A wide range of citizenship law amendments was implemented between 2006 and 2015. Among other things, a new citizenship guide with greater emphasis on Canadian history was issued. Initiatives against the fraudulent acquisition of citizenship were adopted. A new and more demanding citizenship test was introduced, and the language requirements for citizenship were tightened. New and stricter requirements of physical presence in Canada, as a prerequisite for naturalization, were also introduced. According to the Canadian government, these changes were intended to enhance the value of Canadian citizenship. However, the changes have been criticized in both practical and ideological terms. For instance, the naturalization process has become longer and more cumbersome.[45] A new law that made it possible to strip citizenship from Canadian dual citizens convicted of terrorism, treason, or spying offences was also heavily criticized. In a heated exchange during the 2015 election campaign, the leader of the Liberal Party, Justin Trudeau, claimed that the law devalued the citizenship of every Canadian and reminded then Prime Minister Stephen Harper that "a Canadian is a Canadian is a Canadian."[46] Not surprisingly, the new Liberal government revoked the controversial measure a few months after entering office in 2015. To justify the change, the immigration minister stated, "We do not need an additional set of rules that would create two classes of citizens."[47] Nevertheless, most of the amendments adopted between 2006 and 2015 can be seen as pragmatic attempts to develop a stronger commitment to Canada among prospective citizens.

In addition, when data during the early 2000s indicated declining employment success for immigrants in Canada, intensive efforts were made to maximize the proportion of high-skilled immigrants selected on economic grounds. Moreover, greater emphasis in the selection process was placed on prearranged employment and on occupational demand factors.[48] According to Statistics Canada, very recent immigrants have the most difficulty integrating into the labour market. In 2006, the national unemployment rate for immigrants who landed in Canada between 2001 and 2006 was 11.5 per cent, more than double the rate of 4.9 per cent for the Canadian-born population.[49] The increased focus on high-skilled economic immigrants is clearly evident (see Figure 4 in chapter 1). In 2003, family class immigrants accounted for 61.5 per cent of all immigrants while economic immigrants amounted to 47.2 per cent. By 2013, economic immigrants accounted for more than 60 per cent. From a longer-term perspective, the proportion arriving as economic immigrants to Canada has increased from 27 per cent in 1983 to 67 per cent in 2010; the proportion arriving in the family class category declined from 55 per cent to 21 per cent; and the proportion entering as refugees declined from 28 per cent to 9 per cent over the same period.[50] The employability of immigrants is an important reason why so many Canadians believe immigration makes a positive contribution to Canada.[51] The increased focus on high-skilled economic immigrants is a pragmatic and self-interested adaptation of the Canadian model to ever-changing employment needs that regards immigrants as positive resources for Canada.

The pragmatic adaptability of the Canadian model will also have consequences for its international reputation, according to Reitz. He contends that other countries should take these newly emerging Canadian problems and policy changes into account because "they may wonder if the traditional 'Canadian model' still exists; and they may also find it particularly interesting to consider how Canadians are responding to both new realities and to lessons they have learned from their own past experience."[52]

The Canadian model is in many ways a product of pragmatic considerations related to the needs and requirements of the larger projects of nation-building and economic development. The 1960s and the 1970s were particularly noteworthy for immigration legislation with the shift from nation-building as an end in itself to the recognition that labour market development was central to Canada's economic growth and global recognition.[53] Canadian immigration policy has therefore been referred to as "an important economic tool within a social policy framework."[54] The policies of multiculturalism were also introduced and used in a pragmatic fashion to soften the tensions between English-speaking and French-speaking Canadians. As Kymlicka states, "The formula that gradually emerged – namely, multiculturalism within a bilingual framework – was essentially a bargain to ensure white ethnic support for the more urgent task of accommodating Quebec. And, indeed, it has proven to be a very stable bargain."[55] These pragmatic aspects of the Canadian model where focus is put on practical results and concerns are often overlooked. Instead, the model is often discussed in terms of theories or ideological principles related to multiculturalism.

Given the long and strong tradition of political pragmatism and flexibility in Scandinavia, Canada's pragmatic adaptation of its model to changing national and international circumstances will be met with understanding and acceptance. After all, Scandinavian countries are not strangers to pragmatic innovations when it comes to reforming macro-level policies. The transformation of the Scandinavian welfare state systems is illustrative. Substantial reforms were initiated in response to the economic crisis and recession that hit Scandinavia in the early 1990s.[56] With the rise in unemployment, the demands on the welfare state increased at the same time as revenue from taxes fell. In response to increasing budget deficits – Sweden was running the largest budget deficit in the OECD and interest payments amounted to 80 per cent of GDP in 1996 – welfare programs were reassessed. Subsequently, reforms were made: benefit levels were reduced, claim periods were shortened, and eligibility requirements were tightened. The privatization of social service delivery was also initiated, although programs were still funded by the state. While many argued that the changes would culminate in the death of the generous Swedish and Scandinavian welfare state, Hilson accurately observes that "these cuts were generally part of a pragmatic, short-term response to economic difficulties, rather than a comprehensive program for reform."[57] However, the Scandinavian welfare systems remain more generous than those of most countries, and they are still perceived as enviable internationally. As has been indicated, the Scandinavian countries are currently reassessing their immigration and integration policies in a similar pragmatic fashion to ensure the survival of the welfare state to which these policies are linked. Just like Canada's immigration and integration policy model, the emergence of the Scandinavian welfare state models should be seen as pragmatic solutions to practical problems and not results of theoretical design: "Its dynamics change as needs and opportunities are placed on the policy agenda."[58] As Rothstein argues, the long-time survival of the Scandinavian welfare states depends on the "capacity to learn, to handle uncertainty, and to adapt to new conditions."[59] The same seems to apply when it comes to the future of the Canadian immigration and integration policy model.

The increased reliance on temporary foreign workers seems more problematic for the international reputation of the Canadian immigration and integration policy model. Although the reliance on temporary migrants has been a long tradition in Canada – the first program was established in 1966 and it invited Caribbean citizens to work in Canada's agricultural industry – the total number of workers was historically relatively small. In its first year of operation, 264 Jamaican farm workers travelled to labour in the Canadian agricultural industry. By 2008, the number of temporary migrants had reached 250,000.[60]

On the one hand, a heavy reliance on low-skilled temporary migrants represents a continuation of the Canadian model in the sense that it responds to economic demands and pragmatic necessities. The high number of low-skilled migrants can be justified because demand is currently high in Canadian businesses for low-skilled workers. Their temporary status means that these workers will return once demand declines. On the other hand, however, Lenard and Straehle insist that it is "deeply misleading" to claim that the turn to temporary labour migration is consistent with Canada's historical immigration trajectory for at least three reasons.[61] First, decisions about admission to Canada have historically been made by Citizenship and Immigration Canada, which has been guided both by the need to meet the economic demands imposed by the nation's labour market, and by a subjective sense of who can best contribute to the Canadian political community. By contrast, temporary labour migration programs, as they are constructed, have put the choice of admitted migrants almost entirely in the hands of prospective employers. Second, historically immigrants to Canada have been thought of as what Lenard and Straehle refer to as "proto-Canadians," that is, individuals who will soon become Canadian citizens.[62] As such, immigrants have not only been provided with resources in order to enable their integration but have also been welcomed as full contributors to the Canadian community upon admission. The same cannot be said of temporary labour migrants, even though many who first enter on temporary visas do manage to transition to permanent status. Third, according to Lenard and Straehle, temporary labour migration reintroduces, albeit implicitly, a racial dimension to Canadian immigration that the state was proud to dismiss in the mid-1960s. Although temporary labour migrants can originate from anywhere in the world, in practice they come from poor nations and are often racially and ethnically distinct from the still largely white Canadian population. Thus, although the Canadian immigration system has for the past half decade tried explicitly to remove race as an element in Canadian immigration, temporary labour migrations have reintroduced it; "now, the poorest migrants are racially distinct."[63]

Several of the Scandinavian policy experts, civil servants, and politicians interviewed support the impression that Canada's increased reliance on foreign temporary labour migrants represents a radical shift and deviation from the heretofore-reputable Canadian immigration and integration model. One interviewee claims that there is a fundamental contradiction between a humanistic-motivated multicultural policy and the policy towards temporary foreign workers:

> Oil companies in the West have organized the work based on a rotational logic where people are allowed to be in the country for one year and then to be kicked out. Then, when they have been out for six months they are invited back for another year. Just when people have started to establish lasting collectives they are broken off. I consider it to be a calculated cynical policy ... The politics towards temporary workers is something of the most swinish I have encountered ... it does not fit with the wider [Canadian] model.[64]

Canada's increased reliance on foreign temporary workers is indeed problematic. From the perspective of the individual temporary migrants operating at the margins of Canadian society, they are often more easily victims of discrimination and exploitation.[65] However, temporary migrants may also create problems for Canada. One such problem is that temporary migrants, who eventually transition to permanent status, fail to integrate economically and socially into Canadian society due to the lack of access to integration services early on.[66] Another potential problem is that temporary workers may overstay their visas and become permanent undocumented or "non-status" immigrants in Canada.[67] Both these problems can challenge the international reputation of the Canadian immigration and integration policy model in Scandinavia and elsewhere. Consequent to widespread criticism, the Conservative government conducted a systematic review of Canada's Temporary Foreign Worker Program, and a number of reforms were introduced in 2014.[68] Among others, reforms were made to better protect temporary foreign workers from abuse. However, the minister of employment, workforce development and labour in the new Liberal government, MaryAnn Mihychuk, signalled a new "serious review of the whole program."[69] The final outcome of this process is still uncertain.

Canada's declining acceptance of refugees was another worrisome trend for the future of the Canadian model as an international model (see Figure 4 in chapter 1). Canada has a strong international reputation for treating immigrants as a resource. In many countries, immigration is increasingly seen as a problem that burdens public finances or social order due to the lack of integration in the labour market. This is true in Scandinavia, which blocked labour immigration for several decades and instead concentrated on receiving refugees and their families, to the point that the words "refugee" and "immigrant" were used almost synonymously. The situation was drastically different in Canada, which focused on recruiting economic immigrants. The large number of economic immigrants, by contributing to the economy, eliminated the stigma of being an immigrant and helped to finance a significant number of refugees. As a result, Canada was perceived to have a very advantageous "mix of immigrants."[70] Inspired by Canada, the Scandinavian countries rediscovered the positive side to labour immigration from countries outside the EEA and EU. At the same time, the Scandinavian countries are increasingly questioning the "Canadian mix" due to the decline in refugees admitted to Canada compared with economic immigrants.[71] However, the newly elected Liberal government's decision to receive 25,000 Syrian refugees – some of whom were welcomed at the airport by Prime Minister Trudeau himself – was widely publicized in Scandinavia and internationally and contributed positively to Canada's international reputation. Furthermore, the Liberal government's renaming of Citizenship and Immigration Canada (CIC) to Immigration, Refugees, and Citizenship Canada (IRCC) indicates that refugees will be high on the political agenda in years to come.

The future of the Canadian model as an inspirational model in Scandinavia and elsewhere depends on whether its image of treating immigrants as a positive resource appears credible. As a high-ranking Swedish civil-servant reminds us: "We have an international obligation to receive refugees and we need foreign labour, but we would also like that the immigrants stay, build a home, feel at home and become citizens – it is to achieve this we look to Canada."[72]

The continued international reputation of the Canadian immigration and integration policy model is important for several reasons, and the stakes are high for Canada, but also internationally. First, the Canadian immigration and integration policy model has played a crucial role in the promotion of a greater understanding and appreciation internationally of Canada, which is one of the main goals of Canada's foreign policy. The extent to which Canada's image as a "diversity friendly" country has yielded economic advantages, either directly or indirectly, is difficult or impossible to determine exactly. However, it is reasonable to believe that in a globalized world where Canada is competing for tourists, skilled immigrants, and foreign investors, its international image has produced a competitive advantage.[73] Second, the future reputation of the Canadian model internationally is also important from a domestic perspective. Thus, Kymlicka asserts that the international praise of the Canadian model serves to discredit Quebec nationalists: "If the rest of the world is declaring Canadian federalism a success in accommodating diversity, then Quebec separatists, who declare it an oppressive failure, appear as radical ideologues living in a nationalist myth disconnected from reality."[74] International acclaim may also disarm domestic critics of multiculturalism in Canada. Internationally, Canada's image as a peaceful and prosperous multicultural society provides hope to countries experiencing dissatisfaction or problems related to immigration and integration. Just as the Scandinavian countries have acted as role models for others in so many areas of public policy, Canada has acted as an inspirational model in the area of immigration and integration policy.

Policy transfer is not the only source of policy development in Scandinavia, and Canada is not the only inspiration. However, the overall conclusion is that the Canadian immigration and integration policy model is still an internationally recognized model that has shaped and continues to shape reform debates and processes in Denmark, Norway, and Sweden. The model's future relevance for Scandinavia and elsewhere will largely be dependent on its pragmatic adaptation to changing circumstances while being perceived as producing beneficial results for both Canada and its immigrants.

The Scandinavian countries will continue to seek lessons from abroad. While lack of ideological compatibility between countries can be a major constraint to policy transfer,[75] Scandinavian political pragmatism where emphasis is placed on practical concerns and outcomes will support an ongoing quest for policy inspiration at home as well as elsewhere.

Notes

Chapter 1

1 Stein Rokkan, "Immigranterna och det etablerade partisystemet," in *Identitet och minoritet*, ed. David Schwarz (Stockholm: Almqvist & Wiksell, 1971), 222 (my translation).
2 Hudson Strode, *Sweden: Model for a World* (New York: Harcourt, Brace, 1949), 350. Despite its title, Strode is quick to remind the readers of the Scandinavian resemblances: "So in this book when I say Swedish, the reader may in generalities be pleased to substitute the word Scandinavian," xvii.
3 "The Next Supermodel," *The Economist*, 2 February 2013, 9.
4 Mary Hilson, *The Nordic Model: Scandinavia since 1945* (London: Reaktion Books, 2008).
5 Marquis Childs, *Sweden: The Middle Way* (New Haven, CT: Yale University Press, 1936).
6 Eric S. Einhorn and John Logue, "The Scandinavian Democratic Model," *Scandinavian Political Studies* 3 (1986); Lars Mjøset, "The Nordic Model Never Existed, but Does It Have a Future?" *Scandinavian Studies* 64, no. 4 (1992): 652–71.
7 John Helliwell, Richard Layard, and Jeffrey Sachs, *World Happiness Report 2013* (New York: Sustainable Development Solutions Network, 2013); Klaus Schwab, *The Global Competitiveness Report 2013–2014: Insight Report* (Geneva: World Economic Forum, 2013).
8 Neil Elder, Alastair H Thomas, and David Arter, *The Consensual Democracies? The Government and Politics of the Scandinavian States* (Oxford and New York: Blackwell, 1988).
9 Strode, *Sweden: Model for a World*, xx.

10 Government of Scotland, "Scotland's Future: Your Guide to an
Independent Scotland" (Edinburgh: The Scottish Government, 2013), 152.
11 Michael Keating and Malcolm Harvey, *Small Nations in a Big World: What
Scotland Can Learn?* (Edinburgh: Luath Press, 2014).
12 Henry Milner, "The Prospects for Scandinavian-Style Social Democracy in
Quebec/Canada: Proceedings from the Second International Conference
of the Nordic Association for Canadian Studies, University of Lund, 1987,"
in *Canada and the Nordic Countries*, ed. Jørn Carlsen and Bengt Streijfferts
(Lund: Lund University Press, 1988), 227–46.
13 See for instance Dezsö Horváth and Donald J. Daly, "Small Countries in
the World Economy: The Case of Sweden – What Can Canada Learn from
the Swedish Experience" (Halifax, NS: Institute for Research on Public
Policy, 1989); Stéphane Paquin and Pier-Luc Lévesque, *Social-démocratie
2.0: le Québec comparé aux pays scandinaves* (Montreal: Les Presses de
l'Université de Montréal, 2014); Marie-France Raynault, Dominique Côté,
and Sébastien Chartrand, *Le bon sens à la scandinave: politiques et inégalités
sociales de santé* (Montreal: Presses de l'Université de Montréal, 2013).
14 Christine Ingebritsen, *Scandinavia in World Politics* (Lanham: Rowman &
Littlefield, 2006).
15 See for instance Knut Heidar, *Nordic Politics: Comparative Perspectives* (Oslo:
Universitetsforlaget, 2004).
16 Eric S. Einhorn and John Logue, *Modern Welfare States: Scandinavian Politics
and Policy in the Global Age* (New York: Praeger, 2003).
17 The Canadian Scandinavian population was estimated at approximately
108,000 in 1911. See Ninette Kelley and Michael Trebilcock, *The Making of
the Mosaic: A History of Canadian Immigration Policy* (Toronto: University
of Toronto Press, 2010). It should, however, be noted that these figures
include the sizeable emigration from Finland and Iceland.
18 J.S. Woodsworth, *Strangers within Our Gates: Or, Coming Canadians*
(Toronto: F.C. Stephenson, 1909), 92.
19 Grete Brochmann and Anniken Hagelund, *Immigration Policy and the
Scandinavian Welfare State 1945–2010* (Basingstoke: Palgrave Macmillan, 2012).
20 Hilson, *The Nordic Model: Scandinavia since 1945*.
21 The exception here is Swedish speakers in Finland, which comprise 5.4
per cent of the overall population. See Peter Kivisto and Östen Wahlbeck,
Debating Multicultualism in the Nordic Welfare States (Basingstoke: Palgrave
Macmillan, 2013).
22 Harald Runblom, "Immigration to Scandinavia after World War II," in
Ethnicity and Nation Building in the Nordic World, ed. Sven Tägil (London:
Hurst & Company, 1995), 282–324.

23 Silje Vatne Pettersen and Lars Østby, *Skandinavisk komparativ statistikk om integrering: innvandrere i Norge, Sverige og Danmark.*

24 Grete Brochmann and Anniken Hagelund, "Migrants in the Scandinavian Welfare State," *Nordic Journal of Migration Research* 1, no. 1 (2011): 13–24; Brochmann and Hagelund, *Immigration Policy and the Scandinavian Welfare State 1945–2010.*

25 René Cuperus, Karl Duffek, and Johannes Kandel, *The Challenge of Diversity: European Social Democracy Facing Migration, Integration and Multiculturalism* (Innsbruck: Studien Verlag, 2003).

26 Grete Brochmann, "Citizens of Multicultural States," in *The Multicultural Challenge,* ed. Grete Brochmann (Oxford: Elsevier, 2003), 1–11, 6.

27 OECD, *International Migration Outlook 2012* (Paris: OECD Publishing, 2012), http://dx.doi.org/10.1787/migr_outlook-2012-en.

28 Keith Banting and Will Kymlicka, eds., *Multiculturalism and the Welfare State: Recognition and Redistribution in Contemporary Democracies,* 1st ed. (Oxford: Oxford University Press, 2006).

29 Brochmann, "Citizens of Multicultural States."

30 Ingebritsen, *Scandinavia in World Politics,* 93.

31 Brochmann and Hagelund, *Immigration Policy and the Scandinavian Welfare State 1945–2010,* 18.

32 Strode, *Sweden: Model for a World.*

33 Yngve Lithman, "Norwegian Multicultural Debates in a Scandinavian Comparative Perspective," in *Debating Multiculturalism in the Nordic Welfare States,* ed. Peter Kivisto and Östen Wahlbeck (Basingstoke: Palgrave Macmillan, 2013), 246–69.

34 Janice Gross Stein et al., *Uneasy Partners: Multiculturalism and Rights in Canada* (Waterloo, ON: Wilfrid Laurier University Press, 2007).

35 John Ibbitson, "Let Sleeping Dogs Lie," in Stein et al., *Uneasy Partners,* 49–69, 57.

36 Richard Ford, *Canada* (New York: Ecco, 2012), 396.

37 Brochmann and Hagelund, *Immigration Policy and the Scandinavian Welfare State 1945–2010,* 250.

38 James D. Fearon, "Ethnic and Cultural Diversity by Country," *Journal of Economic Growth* 8, no. 2 (2003): 195–222.

39 Leslie S. Laczko, "Canada's Pluralism in Comparative Perspective," *Ethnic and Racial Studies* 17, no. 1 (1994): 20–41; Will Kymlicka, "The Canadian Model of Diversity in a Comparative Perspective," in *Multiculturalism and the Canadian Constitution,* ed. Stephen Tierney (Vancouver: UBC Press, 2007), 61–90; Will Kymlicka, "Disentangling the Debate," in Stein et al., *Uneasy Partners,* 137–56.

40 Patricia Daenzer, Paul van Aerschot, and Tim Rees, "Integration and the Protection of Immigrants: Canadian-Nordic Comparisons," in *The Integration and Protection of Immigrants: Canadian and Scandinavian Critiques*, eds. Paul Van Aerschot and Patricia Daenzer (Burlington, VT: Ashgate, 2014), 213–22.

41 Keith Banting, "Is There a Progressive's Dilemma in Canada? Immigration, Multiculturalism and the Welfare State," *Canadian Journal of Political Science/Revue Canadienne de Science Politique* 43, no. 4 (2010): 797–820.

42 Ibid.

43 Yasmeen Abu-Laban and Christina Gabriel, *Selling Diversity: Immigration, Multiculturalism, Employment Equity, and Globalization* (Peterborough, ON: Broadview Press, 2002).

44 Statistics Canada, "Definitions, Data Sources and Methods," 2008, http://www.statcan.gc.ca/concepts/index-eng.htm.

45 Statistics Canada, "Immigration and Ethnocultural Diversity in Canada," National Household Survey, 2011, http://www12.statcan.gc.ca/nhs-enm/2011/as-sa/99-010-x/99-010-x2011001-eng.pdf.

46 Ibid.

47 Will Kymlicka, "Marketing Canadian Pluralism in the International Arena," *International Journal* 59, no. 4 (2004): 829–52.

48 Stephen J. Tierney, "Introduction: Constitution Building in a Multicultural State," in *Multiculturalism and the Canadian Constitution*, ed. Stephen Tierney (Vancouver: UBC Press, 2007), 3–23.

49 Keith Banting, "Transatlantic Convergence? The Archaeology of Immigrant Integration in Canada and Europe," *International Journal: Canada's Journal of Global Policy Analysis* 69, no. 1 (2014): 66–84.

50 Kymlicka, "The Canadian Model of Diversity."

51 Edward A. Koning and Keith Banting, "The Canadian Model of Immigration and Welfare," in NOU 2011: 7 - *Velferd og migrasjon: den norske modellens framtid*, 2011, 354–71.

52 Oliver Schmidke, "Einwanderungsland Kanada – Ein Vorbild Für Deutschland?," *Aus Politik Und Zeitgeschichte* 44 (2009): 25–32.

53 Triadafilos Triadafilopoulos, "A Model for Europe? A Critical Appraisal of Canadian Integration Policies," in *Politische Steuerung von Integrationsprozessen*, eds. Karen Schönwälder, Sigrid Baringhorst, and Uwe Hunger (Wiesbaden: Verlag für Sozialwissenschaften, 2006), 79–94.

54 Jeffrey G. Reitz, "The Distinctiveness of Canadian Immigration Experience," *Patterns of Prejudice* 46, no. 5 (2012): 518–38.

55 See for instance, Rogers Brubaker, *Citizenship and Nationhood in France and Germany* (Cambridge: Harvard University Press, 1992); Christian Joppke,

Immigration and the Nation-State: The United States, Germany and Great Britain (Oxford and New York: Oxford University Press, 1999).

56 Charles A. Lave and James G. March, *An Introduction to Models in Social Sciences* (Lanham, MD: University Press of America, 1993), 3.

57 Christophe Bertossi, "National Models of Integration in Europe: A Comparative and Critical Analysis," *American Behavioral Scientist* 55, no. 12 (2011): 1561–80.

58 Government of Canada, "Guide to the Private Sponsorship of Refugees Program," 1 November 2003, http://www.cic.gc.ca/english/resources/publications/ref-sponsor/section-2.asp.

59 Kymlicka, "Disentangling the Debate."

60 Reitz, "The Distinctiveness of Canadian Immigration Experience."

61 Banting and Kymlicka, *Multiculturalism and the Welfare State.*

62 Kymlicka, "The Canadian Model of Diversity in a Comparative Perspective."

63 The most important exceptions concern recently arrived elderly immigrants, family-class immigrants under sponsorship agreements, and temporary foreign workers (see Banting, "Is There a Progressive's Dilemma in Canada?").

64 This is not always the case at the provincial level. For instance, issues related to ethnic diversity were central in the debate leading up to the Quebec election in 2014. See for instance Trygve Ugland, "The Quebec Charter of Values: A Solution in Search of Problems," *Journal of Eastern Townships Studies* 42 (2014): 11–21.

65 Inder Marwah, Triadafilos Triadafilopoulos, and Stephen White, "Immigration, Citizenship and Canada's New Conservative Party," in *Conservatism in Canada*, ed. David M. Rayside and James Harold Farney (Toronto: University of Toronto Press, 2013), 95–119.

66 Reitz, "The Distinctiveness of Canadian Immigration Experience." The exception is here the 2015 election, when resettlement of Syrian refugees became a defining issue. While all the main political parties promised increased efforts, the election resulted in a new majority Liberal government led by Justin Trudeau, who had significantly exceeded the competing parties' promises for assistance. See Shauna Labman, "Private Sponsorship: Complementary or Conflicting Interests?," *Refuge: Canada's Journal on Refugees* 32, no. 2 (2016): 67–80.

67 Marwah, Triadafilopoulos, and White, "Immigration, Citizenship and Canada's New Conservative Party," 95–6.

68 Citizenship and Immigration Canada, *CIC Annual Tracking Survey – Winter 2010 Final Report* (Ottawa: Ekos Research, April 2010).

69 Reitz, "The Distinctiveness of Canadian Immigration Experience," 518.
70 Don J. DeVoretz, Sergiy Pivnenko, and Morton Beiser, "The Economic Experiences of Refugees in Canada," in *Homeland Wanted: Interdisciplinary Perspective on Refugee Settlement in the West,* eds. Peter Waxman and Val Colic-Peisker (New York: Nova Science Publishers, 2004), 1–21.
71 Citizenship and Immigration Canada (CIC) was renamed as Immigration, Refugees and Citizenship Canada (IRCC) in November 2015. This book refers to the original name, CIC, in discussions of events prior to this date.
72 Kymlicka, "The Canadian Model of Diversity," 62.
73 It should also be mentioned that Canadian policies themselves might be affected by these international activities. Sandy Irvine suggests that the reform of Canadian refugee policies during the 1990s was partly due to the socialization of Canadian bureaucrats participating in transnational government networks. See J.A. Sandy Irvine, "Canadian Refugee Policy and the Role of International Bureaucratic Networks in Domestic Paradigm Change," in *Policy Paradigms, Transnationalism and Domestic Politics,* ed. Grace Skogstad (Toronto: University of Toronto Press, 2011), 171–201.
74 Similar observations have been made with reference to the emergence of the so-called Dutch multicultural model. For instance, Duyvendak and Scholten talk about a "coproduction" of the model by researchers and policy-makers. See Jan Willem Duyvendak and Peter Scholten, "Beyond the Dutch 'Multicultural Model': The Coproduction of Integration Policy Frames," *Journal of International Migration and Integration* 12 (2011): 331–48.
75 Kymlicka, "The Canadian Model of Diversity in a Comparative Perspective," 85.
76 Kymlicka, "Marketing Canadian Pluralism."
77 Abu-Laban and Gabriel, *Selling Diversity.*
78 Harald Bauder, Patti Tamara Lenard, and Christine Straehle, "Lessons from Canada and Germany: Immigration and Integration Experiences Compared," *Comparative Migration Studies* 2, no. 1 (2014): 1–7, 2.
79 Reitz, "The Distinctiveness of Canadian Immigration Experience."
80 Kymlicka, "The Canadian Model of Diversity."
81 David Dolowitz and David Marsh, "Who Learns What from Whom: A Review of the Policy Transfer Literature," *Political Studies* 44, no. 2 (1996): 343–57; David Dolowitz and David Marsh, "Learning from Abroad: The Role of Policy Transfer in Contemporary Policy-Making," *Governance* 13, no. 1 (2000): 5–23; David Dolowitz, "Learning by Observing: Surveying the International Arena," *Policy & Politics* 37, no. 3 (2009): 317–34.

82 Michael Sinclair, "Canadian Involvement in the Brain Drain from Africa: Opportunities for Action," *Issue: A Journal of Opinion* 9, no. 4 (1 December 1979): 19–25.

83 Patti Tamara Lenard and Christine Straehle, *Legislated Inequality: Temporary Labour Migration in Canada* (Montreal: McGill-Queen's University Press, 2012).

84 Alan Cairns, *Citizens Plus: Aboriginal Peoples and the Canadian State* (Vancouver: UBC Press, 2011).

85 Neil Bissoondath, *Selling Illusions: The Cult of Multiculturalism in Canada* (Toronto: Penguin Books, 2002).

86 Phil Ryan, *Multicultiphobia* (Toronto: University of Toronto Press, 2010).

87 See for instance Christian Joppke, "The Retreat of Multiculturalism in the Liberal State: Theory and Policy," *British Journal of Sociology* 55, no. 2 (2004): 237–57.

88 CBC News Poll on Discrimination, November 2014: http://s3.documentcloud. org/documents/1362391/cbc-discrimination-poll-november-2014.pdf.

89 Ibid.

90 Alain-G Gagnon and Raffaele Iacovino, *Federalism, Citizenship, and Quebec: Debating Multinationalism* (Toronto: University of Toronto Press, 2007).

91 Alain-G Gagnon and Raffaele Iacovino, "Interculturalism: Expanding the Boundaries of Citizenship," in *Democracy, Nationalism and Multiculturalism*, ed. Ramón Máiz and Ferrán Requejo (New York: Frank Cass Publishers, 2005), 25–42.

92 Marie Mc Andrew et al., "L'aptitude au Français des élèves montréalais d'origine immigrée: impact de la densité ethnique de l'école, du taux de francisation associé à la langue maternelle et de l'ancienneté d'implantation," *Cahiers Québécois de Démographie* 29, no. 1 (2000): 89–117.

93 Quoted in Gagnon and Iacovino, "Interculturalism," 30.

94 Marie Mc Andrew, "Quebec Immigration, Integration and Intercultural Policy: A Critical Assessment," *Indian Journal of Federal Studies* 15, no. 1 (2007): 1–18.

95 Ibid., 11.

96 Ugland, "The Quebec Charter of Values."

97 Government of Quebec, *Bill 60 – Charter Affirming the Values of State Secularism and Religious Neutrality and of Equality between Women and Men, and Providing a Framework for Accommodation Requests* (Quebec: Québec Official Publisher, 2013), 6.

98 Ugland, "The Quebec Charter of Values."

99 Marwah, Triadafilopoulos, and White, "Immigration, Citizenship and Canada's New Conservative Party," 95–6.

100 Eleanor D. Westney, *Imitation and Innovation: The Transfer of Western Organizational Patterns to Meiji Japan* (Cambridge: Harvard University Press, 1987).
101 Patrick Dunleavy and Chrisopher Hood, "From Old Public Administration to New Public Management," *Public Money & Management* 14, no. 3 (1994): 9–16.
102 Dolowitz and Marsh, "Learning from Abroad," 5.
103 Ibid.
104 Herbert Obinger, Carina Schmitt, and Peter Starke, "Policy Diffusion and Policy Transfer in Comparative Welfare State Research," *Social Policy & Administration* 47, no. 1 (2013): 111–29.
105 Stefanie Ettelt, Nicholas Mays, and Ellen Nolte, "Policy Learning from Abroad: Why It Is More Difficult than It Seems," *Policy & Politics* 40, no. 4 (2012): 491–504.
106 Christine Ingebritsen refers to the Scandinavian countries as global agenda setters. Ingebritsen, *Scandinavia in World Politics*.
107 See for instance George Hoberg, "Sleeping with an Elephant: The American Influence on Canadian Environmental Regulation," *Journal of Public Policy* 11, no. 1 (1991): 107–31; Michael Howlett and Sima Joshi-Koop, "Transnational Learning, Policy Analytical Capacity, and Environmental Policy Convergence: Survey Results from Canada," *Global Environmental Change* 21, no. 1 (2011): 85–92; David A. Rochefort and Paula Goering, "'More a Link than a Division': How Canada Has Learned from U.S. Mental Health Policy," *Health Affairs* 17, no. 5 (1998): 110–27; Colin J. Bennett, "How States Utilize Foreign Evidence," *Journal of Public Policy* 11, no. 1 (1991): 31–54.
108 Richard Rose, *Lesson-Drawing in Public Policy: A Guide to Learning across Time and Space* (Chatham: Chatham House Publishers, 1993); David Brian Robertson and Jerold L. Waltman, "The Politics of Policy Borrowing," in *Something Borrowed, Something Learned?: The Transatlantic Market in Education and Training Reform*, ed. David Finegold, Laurel McFarland, and William Richardson (Washington, DC: Brookings Institution, 1993), 21–44.
109 Rose, "What Is Lesson-Drawing?"
110 Government of Canada, "Annual Report on the Operation of the Canadian Multiculturalism Act 2011–2012: Promoting Integration" (Ottawa: Citizenship and Immigration Canada, 2012), 9.
111 See for instance Paul Pierson, *Politics in Time: History, Institutions, and Social Analysis* (Princeton: Princeton University Press, 2004); Christopher Pollitt, *Time, Policy, Management: Governing with the Past* (Oxford: Oxford University Press, 2008); Simon Bulmer, "Politics in Time Meets the Politics

of Time: Historical Institutionalism and the EU Timescape," *Journal of European Public Policy* 16, no. 2 (2009): 307–24.

112 Diane Stone, "Learning Lessons and Transferring Policy across Time, Space and Disciplines," *Politics* 19, no. 1 (1999): 51–9; Mauricio I. Dussauge-Laguna, "The Neglected Dimension: Bringing Time Back into Cross-National Policy Transfer Studies," *Policy Studies* 33, no. 6 (2012): 567–85.

113 Dolowitz and Marsh, "Who Learns What from Whom"; David Benson and Andrew Jordan, "What Have We Learned from Policy Transfer Research? Dolowitz and Marsh Revisited," *Political Studies Review* 9, no. 3 (2011): 366–78.

114 Robert F. Rich, "Measuring Knowledge Utilization: Processes and Outcomes," *Knowledge and Policy* 10, no. 3 (1997): 11–24.

115 Rose, "What Is Lesson-Drawing?"; Rose, *Lesson-Drawing in Public Policy*; Dolowitz and Marsh, "Learning from Abroad."

116 Harold Wolman, "Understanding Cross National Policy Transfers: The Case of Britain and the US," *Governance* 5, no. 1 (1992): 27–45.

117 Westney, *Imitation and Innovation*.

118 Dussauge-Laguna, "The Neglected Dimension," 578.

119 Colin J. Bennett, "What Is Policy Convergence and What Causes It?," *British Journal of Political Science* 21, no. 2 (1991), 219.

120 Dolowitz and Marsh, "Learning from Abroad."

121 Mark Evans and Jonathan Davies, "Understanding Policy Transfer: A Multilevel, Multi-Disciplinary Perspective," *Public Administration* 77, no. 2 (1999): 361–85.

122 Dong Lisheng, Tom Christensen, and Martin Painter, "A Case Study of China's Administrative Reform: The Importation of the Super-Department," *American Review of Public Administration* 40, no. 2 (2010): 170–88.

123 Rose, *Lesson-Drawing in Public Policy*.

124 Johan P. Olsen and B. Guy Peters, *Lessons from Experience: Experiential Learning in Administrative Reforms in Eight Democracies* (Oslo: Scandinavian University Press, 1996).

125 Dolowitz and Marsh, "Learning from Abroad."

126 Benson and Jordan, "What Have We Learned from Policy Transfer Research?"; Dolowitz, "Learning by Observing."

127 Dolowitz and Marsh, "Who Learns What from Whom."

128 Jamie Peck and Nik Theodore, *Fast Policy: Experimental Statecraft at the Threshold of Neoliberalism* (Minneapolis: University of Minnesota Press, 2015).

129 Christophe Bertossi and Jan Willem Duyvendak, "National Models of Integration in Europe: The Costs for Comparative Research," *Comparative European Politics* 10, no. 5 (2012): 237–47; Oliver Schmidke, "Beyond National Models? Governing Migration and Integration at the Regional and Local Levels in Canada and Germany," *Comparative Migration Studies* 2, no. 1 (2014): 77–99; Elke Winter, "Traditions of Nationhood or Political Conjuncture? Debating Citizenship in Canada and Germany," *Comparative Migration Studies* 2, no. 1 (2014): 29–55.

130 Jan Willem Duyvendak and Peter Scholten, "Deconstructing the Dutch Multicultural Model: A Frame Perspective on Dutch Immigrant Integration Policymaking," *Comparative European Politics* 10, no. 3 (2012): 266–82.

131 For a more extensive discussion of migration and convergence theories, see Christian Joppke, *Selecting by Origin: Ethnic Migration in the Liberal State* (Cambridge, MA: Harvard University Press, 2005).

132 Dietrich Thränhardt and Michael Bommes, *National Paradigms of Migration Research* (Göttingen: V & R Unipress, 2010).

133 See for instance Caelesta Poppelaars and Peter W.A. Scholten, "Two Worlds Apart: The Divergence of National and Local Integration Policies in the Netherlands," *Administration and Society* 40, no. 4 (2008): 335–57.

134 Reitz, "The Distinctiveness of Canadian Immigration Experience"; Raffaele Iacovino, "Canadian Federalism and the Governance of Immigration," in *The Politics of Immigration in Multi-Level States* (Basingstoke: Palgrave Macmillan, 2014), 86–107.

135 Andrew Griffith, *Multiculturalism in Canada: Evidence and Anecdote* (Ottawa: Anar Press, 2015).

136 Bertossi and Duyvendak, "National Models of Integration in Europe."

137 Reitz, "The Distinctiveness of Canadian Immigration Experience."

138 See for instance Ruud Koopmans, Paul Statham, Marco Giugni, and Florence Passy, *Contested Citizenship: Immigration and Cultural Diversity in Europe* (Minneapolis: University of Minnesota Press, 2005).

139 Interview Number 30, Ottawa, 7 March 2016.

140 Bertossi, "National Models of Integration in Europe."

141 Peck and Theodore, *Fast Policy*.

142 Ibid., xxiv.

143 Olsen and Peters, *Lessons from Experience*.

144 Tom Christensen, "Modern State Reforms," in *Nordic Politics: Comparative Perspectives*, ed. Knut Heidar (Oslo: Universitetsforlaget, 2004), 24–39.

145 Ibid., 39.

146 Kerstin Sahlin-Andersson, "National, International and Transnational Constructions of New Public Management," in *New Public Management:*

The Transformation of Ideas and Practice, ed. Tom Christensen and Per Lægreid (Aldershot: Ashgate, 2001), 43–72.

147 Tom Christensen et al., *Organization Theory and the Public Sector: Instrument, Culture and Myth* (London: Routledge, 2007).

148 James G. March and Johan P. Olsen, *Rediscovering Institutions: The Organizational Basis of Politics* (New York: Free Press, 1989); Philip Selznick, *Leadership in Administration* (New York: Harper & Row, 1957).

149 Paul J. DiMaggio and Walter W. Powell, "The Iron Cage Revisited: Institutional Isomorphism and Collective Rationality in Organizational Fields," *American Sociological Review* 48 (1983): 147–60; John. W. Meyer and Brian Rowan, "Institutionalized Organizations: Formal Structure as Myth and Ceremony," *American Journal of Sociology* 83, no. 2 (1977): 340–63.

150 Rudolf Klein, "Learning from Others: Shall the Last Be the First?," *Journal of Health Politics, Policy and Law* 22, no. 5 (1997): 1267–78.

151 Ettelt, Mays, and Nolte, "Policy Learning from Abroad."

152 Nils Brunsson, *The Organization of Hypocrisy: Talk, Decisions and Actions in Organizations* (Chichester: John Wiley & Sons, 1989).

153 Thomas J. Anton, "Policy-Making and Political Culture in Sweden," *Scandinavian Political Studies,* no. 4 (1969): 88–102; Einhorn and Logue, *Modern Welfare States.*

154 Åsa Lundqvist and Klaus Petersen, eds., *In Experts We Trust: Knowledge, Politics and Bureaucracy in Nordic Welfare States* (Odense: University Press of Southern Denmark, 2010).

155 Ibid., 20–1.

156 Childs, *Sweden: The Middle Way.*

157 Einhorn and Logue, *Modern Welfare States,* 240.

158 Ibid., 254.

159 Patricia Daenzer, Paul van Aerschot, and Tim Rees, *Integration and the Protection of Immigrants,* 216.

160 James G. March and Johan P. Olsen, "The Institutional Dynamics of International Political Orders," *International Organization* 52, no. 4 (1998): 943–69; James G. March and Johan P. Olsen, "The Logic of Appropriateness," in *The Oxford Handbook of Public Policy,* ed. Michael Moran, Martin Rein, and Robert E. Goodin (Oxford: Oxford University Press, 2006), 689–708.

161 Johan P. Olsen, "Institutional Design in Democratic Contexts," *Journal of Political Philosophy* 5, no. 3 (1997): 203–29.

162 Kymlicka, "The Canadian Model of Diversity in a Comparative Perspective."

163 Gary P. Freeman, "National Models, Policy Types, and the Politics of Immigration in Liberal Democracies," *West European Politics* 29, no. 2 (2006): 227–47.
164 Brochmann and Hagelund, *Immigration Policy and the Scandinavian Welfare State 1945–2010.*
165 See http://ec.europa.eu/eurostat/statistics-explained/ images/1/18/Five_main_citizenships_of_%28non-EU%29_asylum_ applicants%2C_2015_%28number_of_first_time_applicants%2C_ rounded_figures%29_YB16.png.
166 Grete Brochmann and Anne Britt Djuve, "Multiculturalism or Assimilation? The Norwegian Welfare State Approach," in Kivisto and Wahlbeck, *Debating Multiculturalism*, 223.
167 Lithman, "Norwegian Multicultural Debates."
168 Richard Common, *Public Management and Policy Transfer in Southeast Asia* (Aldershot: Ashgate, 2001).
169 Peck and Theodore, *Fast Policy*, 34.
170 Government of Canada, "Annual Report on the Operation of the Canadian Multiculturalism Act 2011–2012," 9.

Chapter 2

1 Interview Number 15, Stockholm, 19 August 2013.
2 Joppke, "The Retreat of Multiculturalism in the Liberal State."
3 Proposition 2007/08:147: *Nya regler för arbetskraftsinvandring* (Stockholm: Riksdagen, 2008).
4 Henrik Emilsson et al., *The World's Most Open Country: Labour Migration to Sweden after the 2008 Law* (Malmö: Malmö Institute for Studies of Migration, Diversity and Welfare, Malmö University, 2014).
5 Karin Borevi, "Sweden: The Flagship of Multiculturalism," in Brochmann and Hagelund, *Immigration Policy and the Scandinavian Welfare State 1945–2010*, 25–96.
6 OECD, *International Migration Outlook 2012.*
7 Proposition 2009/10: 77: *Försörjningskrav vid anhöriginvandring* (Stockholm: Riksdagen, 2010).
8 Borevi, "Sweden: The Flagship of Multiculturalism," 75.
9 Karin Borevi, "Understanding Swedish Multiculturalism," in Kivisto and Wahlbeck, *Debating Multiculturalism*, 140–69.
10 Han Entzinger, "The Rise and Fall of Multiculturalism: The Case of the Netherlands," in *Towards Assimilation and Citizenship: Immigrants in Liberal States*, ed. Christian Joppke and Eva Morawska (Basingstoke: Palgrave,

2003), 59–86; Joppke, "The Retreat of Multiculturalism in the Liberal State."

11 Proposition 1975:26: *Regeringens Proposition om riktlinjer för invandrar- och minoritetspolitiken* (Stockholm: Riksdagen, 1975).

12 Proposition 1999/2000: 147: *Lag om svenskt medborgarskap* (Stockholm: Riksdagen, 2000).

13 Proposition 2013/14:143: *Ett medborgarskap som grundas på samhörighet* (Stockholm: Riksdagen, 2014).

14 Edward A. Koning, "Ethnic and Civic Dealings with Newcomers: Naturalization Policies and Practices in Twenty-Six Immigration Countries," *Ethnic and Racial Studies* 34, no. 11 (2011): 1974–94. As explained by Koning, ultimately the difference between ethnic and civic policies concerns the distinction between policies that set high versus low bars for inclusion.

15 Banting, "Transatlantic Convergence?"

16 Svensk Författningssamling 2008: 567, *Diskrimineringslag* (Stockholm: Sveriges Riksdag, 2008).

17 Ibid., 2 (my translation).

18 Borevi, "Understanding Swedish Multiculturalism."

19 Banting, "Transatlantic Convergence?"

20 Mats Wickström, "The Difference White Ethnics Made: The Multiculturalist Turn of Sweden in Comparison to the Cases of Canada and Denmark," in *Migrations and Welfare States: Policies, Discourses and Institutions*, ed. Heidi Vad Jønsson et al. (Helsinki: NordWel, 2013), 25–58.

21 Rokkan, "Immigranterna och det etablerade partisystemet," 222.

22 Mats Wickström, "Conceptual Change in Postwar Sweden: The Marginalization of Assimilation and the Introduction of Integration," in Kivisto and Wahlbeck, *Debating Multiculturalism*, 131.

23 Henrik Emilsson, "Vad kan vi lära av Kanadas migrations- og integrationspolitik?"(blog post), February 2011, http://integrationsbloggen.blogspot.ca.

24 Petter Hojem and Martin Ådahl, eds., *Kanadamodellen: hur invandring leder till jobb* (Stockholm: Fores, 2011).

25 Ibid., 17 (my translation).

26 Peck and Theodore, *Fast Policy*, xxiv.

27 Interview Number 27, Stockholm, 1 October 2015.

28 SOU 2002:13, *Vår anhöriginvandring* (Stockholm: Regeringskanseliet, 2002).

29 Ibid.

30 Interview Number 15, Stockholm, 19 August 2013.

31 SOU 2005: 50, *Arbetskraftsinvandring till Sverige - befolkningsutveckling, arbetsmarknad i förändring, internationell utblick* (Stockholm: Regeringskanseliet,

2005); SOU 2006: 87, *Arbetskraftsinvandring till Sverige - förslag och konsekvenser* (Stockholm: Regeringskansliet, 2006).

32 SOU 2005: 50, *Arbetskraftsinvandring till Sverige - befolkningsutveckling, arbetsmarknad i förändring, internationell utblick,* 88 (my translation).

33 Ibid., 90 (my translation).

34 Interview Number 27, Stockholm, 1 October 2015.

35 Interview Number 28, Stockholm, 2 October 2015.

36 Interview Number 16, Uppsala, 20 August 2013; Interview Number 27, Stockholm, 1 October 2015; Interview Number 28, Stockholm, 2 October 2015.

37 Interview Number 15, Stockholm, 19 August 2013.

38 Interview Number 30, Ottawa, 7 March 2016.

39 SOU 1997: 162, *Medborgarskap och identitet* (Stockholm: Regeringskanseliet, 1997); SOU 1999: 34, *Svenskt medborgarskap* (Stockholm: Regeringskanseliet, 1999).

40 SOU 2013: 29, *Det svenska medborgarskapet* (Stockholm: Regeringskanseliet, 2013).

41 Interview Number 15, Stockholm, 19 August 2013. Another interesting new development that illustrates the Canadian inspiration is the adoption of Canada's practice of welcoming new citizens on the national day. Citizenship ceremonies take place across the country the entire year, but the special ceremonies organized on Canada Day on July 1 are particularly popular. In 2014, forty-six special citizenship ceremonies were held across the country on Canada Day. A recent development in Sweden is that new citizens receive their citizenship on the national day on June 6.

42 Interview Number 19, Ottawa, 15 April 2014. This is a very high number, but it is important to remember that Scandinavian parliamentarians travel a lot in a comparative perspective. One long overseas and two shorter European travels per parliamentary period seem to be the norm among Swedish parliamentarians.

43 Peter Strand, "Utvärdering av utskottens och EU-nämndens utrikesresor 2010–2013" (Stockholm: Utskottsavdelingen, Utvärderings- och forskningssekretariatet, Sveriges Riksdag, 2013).

44 Interview Number 18, Ottawa, 14 April 2014.

45 Interview Number 28, Stockholm, 2 October 2015.

46 Interview Number 19, Ottawa, 15 April 2014 (my translation).

47 Interview Number 18, Ottawa, 14 April 2014.

48 Government of Canada, "Annual Report on the Operation of the Canadian Multiculturalism Act 2011–2012: Promoting Integration" (Ottawa: Citizenship and Immigration Canada, 2012), 9.

49 Sveriges Riksdag, *Rapport från tredje vice talmansresa till Kanada 31 januari – 4 februari 2011, PM 2011 02 10* (Stockholm: Sveriges Riksdag, 2011).

50 Ibid., 1 (my translation).

51 Interview Number 27, Stockholm, 1 October 2015.

52 Interview Number 31, email, 2 June 2016.

53 Wallenberg was the first in a very exclusive list to be declared an honorary citizen of Canada in 1958.

54 Interview Number 21, email, 17 December 2014.

55 Ministry of Employment, Minnesanteckningar från sr Erik Ullenhags resa till USA och Kanada den 18 – 22 mars 2013, Promemoria A2013/748/IE (Stockholm: Regeringskansliet, 2013).

56 Interview Number 19, Ottawa, 15 April 2014.

57 Susan F. Martin, "International Migration and Global Governance," *Global Summitry* 1, no. 1 (2015): 64–83.

58 Interview Number 15, Stockholm, 19 August 2013; Interview Number 17, Stockholm, 23 August 2013.

59 The IGC is an informal, non-decision-making forum of high-level civil servants. It meets several times annually to debate and exchange intergovernmental information on the management of international migratory flows. The IGC was founded in 1985, and it has a permanent secretariat in Geneva, Switzerland. The United Nations High Commissioner for Refugees, the International Organization for Migration, and the European Commission participate in the IGC in addition to the sixteen member states.

60 Interview Number 15, Stockholm, 19 August 2013.

61 Bennett, *What Is Policy Convergence and What Causes It?* 219.

62 Interview Number 18, Ottawa, 14 April 2014.

63 Emilsson et al., *The World's Most Open Country: Labour Migration to Sweden after the 2008 Law.*

64 Program, International Site Visit to Sweden, concluding in Copenhagen, Leaders' Roundtable on Immigration, The Conference Board of Canada, 2.

65 Ibid., 2.

66 Email, 22 October 2015.

67 Interview Number 28, Stockholm, 2 October 2015.

68 Interview Number 15, Stockholm, 19 August 2013.

69 Pieter Bevelander and Ravi Pendakur, "The Labour Market Integration of Refugee and Family Reunion Immigrants: A Comparison of Outcomes in Canada and Sweden," *Journal of Ethnic and Migration Studies* 40, no. 5 (2014), 690.

70 "Sweden Slams Shut Its Open-Door Policy towards Refugees," *Guardian*, 24 November 2015, http://www.theguardian.com/world/2015/nov/24/sweden-asylum-seekers-refugees-policy-reversal.

71 Government of Sweden, "Sweden's Migration and Asylum Policy: Fact Sheet," February 2017, http://www.government.se/491b3d/contentassets/26536c43ab3b41df90c064c2049b1bce/swedens-migration-and-asylum-policy.

72 Banting, "Transatlantic Convergence?"

Chapter 3

1 Interview Number 13, Copenhagen, 6 May 2013 (my translation).

2 Christoffer Green-Pedersen and Jesper Krogstrup, "Immigration as a Political Issue in Denmark and Sweden," *European Journal of Political Research* 47, no. 5 (2008): 610–34.

3 Eva Østergaard-Nielsen, "Counting the Costs: Denmark's Changing Migration Policies," *International Journal of Urban and Regional Research* 27, no. 2 (2003): 448–54, 449.

4 Government of Denmark, *En ny udlændingepolitik* (Copenhagen: Statsministeriet, 2002).

5 Government of Denmark, *På vej mod en ny integrationspolitik* (Copenhagen: Regeringen, 2002).

6 Government of Denmark, *Regeringens integrations- og udlændingepolitik – status marts 2003* (Copenhagen: Regeringen, 2003).

7 Government of Denmark, *En ny chance til alle: regeringens integrationsplan* (Copenhagen: Ministeriet for Flygtninge, Indvandrere og Integration, 2005).

8 Karen Fog Olwig and Karsten Paerregaard, *The Question of Integration: Immigration, Exclusion and the Danish Welfare State* (Newcastle: Cambridge Scholars Publishing, 2011); Heidi Vad Jønsson and Klaus Petersen, "Denmark: A National Welfare State Meets the World," in Brochmann and Hagelund, *Immigration Policy and the Scandinavian Welfare State 1945–2010*, 97–148; Østergaard-Nielsen, "Counting the Costs."

9 Kim U. Kjær, "The Abolition of the Danish de facto Concept," *International Journal of Refugee Law* 15, no. 2 (2003): 254–75.

10 Mikkel Rytter, "The Family of Denmark and the Aliens: Kinship Images in Danish Integration Policies," in Fog Olwig and Paerregaard, *The Question of Integration*, 54–76.

11 Ibid.

12 Marianne Frank Hansen, Marie Louise Schultz-Nielsen, and Torben Tranæs, "The Fiscal Impact of Immigration to Welfare States of the Scandinavian Type," paper presented at the IZA/Ministry of Finance,

Slovak Republic/Council for Budget Responsibility/CELSI Conference on Fiscal Policy Tools and Labor Markets during the Great Recession, Bratislava, Slovakia, 26–27 October 2015.

13 Ibid.

14 Brochmann and Hagelund, *Immigration Policy and the Scandinavian Welfare State 1945–2010*, 257.

15 Sune Lægaard, "Danish Anti-Multiculturalism? The Significance of the Political Framing of Diversity," in Kivisto and Wahlbeck, *Debating Multiculturalism*, 170–96, 178.

16 The new citizenship law permits immigrants to become Danish citizens without having to give up the citizenship of their own country, and it will also allow Danes who have given up their citizenship for another to be able to reclaim it. The decision to allow dual citizenship is based on a report by an expert panel that was established in 2012. The panel initially looked into the possibility of limiting dual citizenship to citizens from other EU/EEA/EFTA nations or countries in NATO only. However, this solution was abandoned since it was likely to be seen as discriminatory and in conflict with international human rights conventions.

17 However, the permanent residency requirements were lowered to five years in 2010.

18 Østergaard-Nielsen, "Counting the Costs."

19 John Andersen, Jørgen Elm Larsen, and Iver Hornemann Møller, "The Exclusion and Marginalisation of Immigrants in the Danish Welfare Society: Dilemmas and Challenges," *International Journal of Sociology and Social Policy* 29, no. 5/6 (2009): 274–86.

20 Jønsson and Petersen, "Denmark: A National Welfare State Meets the World."

21 Lægaard, "Danish Anti-Multiculturalism?"

22 Ministry of Immigration, Integration and Housing, "The Danish Immigration Authorities Are Informing about Changes of Conditions regarding Residence in Denmark Being Implemented by the New Danish Government" (Letter), 7 September 2015.

23 Ibid.

24 Adam Taylor, "A Danish Politician Explains Why It's Okay to Take Valuables from Refugees," *Washington Post*, 27 January 2016, https://www.washingtonpost.com/news/worldviews/wp/2016/01/27/a-danish-politician-explains-why-its-okay-to-take-valuables-from-refugees.

25 Stefan Kühner, "The Dependent Variable Problem within the Comparative Analysis of the Welfare State Revisited: What If We Waited a Little Longer?," *Social Policy Review 27: Analysis and Debate in Social Policy* (Bristol: Policy Press, 2015).

26 Martin Bak Jørgensen, "Understanding the Research–Policy Nexus in Denmark and Sweden: The Field of Migration and Integration," *British Journal of Politics & International Relations* 13, no. 1 (2011): 93–109.

27 Interview Number 14, Copenhagen, 7 May 2013.

28 Troels Mylenberg, "Weiss: Arbejde er den bedste integration," *Berlingske Tidende*, 21 July 1997, 5 (my translation).

29 Interview Number 24, email, 14 September 2015.

30 Morten Ørtoft, "Mere målrettet integration på vej," *Aktuelt*, 1 October 1997, 3.

31 Interview Number 12, Copenhagen, 6 May 2013.

32 Interview Number 13, Copenhagen, 7 May 2013.

33 Garbi Schmidt, "Law and Identity: Transnational Arranged Marriages and the Boundaries of Danishness," *Journal of Ethnic and Migration Studies* 37, no. 2 (2011): 257–75.

34 Ibid., 259.

35 "Et foregangsland," *Information*, 26 January 2002, http://www.information.dk/65291 (my translation).

36 See Hans Jørgen Nielsen, *Er danskerne fremmedfjendske? Udlandets syn på debatten om indvandrerne 2000–2002* (Aarhus: Aarhus Universitetsforlag, 2004).

37 Council of Europe, *Report by Mr. Alvaro Gil-Robles, Commissioner for Human Rights, on His Visit to Denmark, 13–16 April 2004* (Strasbourg: Council of Europe, 2004), http://www.refworld.org/docid/41596b8d4.html.

38 Ibid., 25.

39 Quoted in Schmidt, "Law and Identity," 261.

40 Interview Number 11, Copenhagen, 6 May 2013; Interview Number 13, Copenhagen, 7 May 2013.

41 Think Tank on Integration in Denmark, *Immigration and Integration Policies in Denmark and Selected Countries* (Copenhagen: Ministry of Refugee, Immigration and Integration Affairs, 2004), 1. Denmark is in this report compared with Canada, Finland, Germany, Italy, the Netherlands, Sweden, and the United Kingdom.

42 Ibid., 17–18.

43 Hans Hansen et al., "Udlændinge- og integrationspolitik i syv udvalgte lande - SFI's bidrag til baggrundsrapport fra Tænketanken om udfordringer for integrationsindsatsen i Danmark" (Copenhagen: Danish National Institute of Social Research, 2004).

44 Tænketanken om Udfordringer for Integrationsindsatsen i Danmark, *Udlændinge- og integrationspolitikken i Danmark og udvalgte lande* (Copenhagen: Ministeriet for Flygtninge, Indvandrere og Integration, 2004), 122 (my translation and my italics).

45 Think Tank on Integration in Denmark, *Immigration and Integration Policies in Denmark and Selected Countries*, 19.

46 Ibid., 20; also Interview Number 11, Copenhagen, 6 May 2013.

47 Velfærdskommissionen, *Fremtidens velfærd - sådan gør andre lande* (Copenhagen: Velfærdskommissionen, 2005), 235 (my translation).

48 Ibid., 255 (my translation).

49 Velfærdskommissionen, *Fremtidens velfærd - vores valg* (Copenhagen: Velfærdskommissionen, 2005).

50 Interview Number 25, Copenhagen, 25 September 2015.

51 Velfærdskommissionen, "Fremtidens velfærd - vores valg," 23 (my translation).

52 Jakob Stig Jørgensen, "Konservative: Indvandrere skal deles op i gode og dårlige," *Politiken*, 14 November 2013, http://politiken.dk/indland/politik/ECE2131527/konservative-indvandrere-skal-deles-op-i-gode-og-daarlige/.

53 Government of Denmark, *Nye tider. Nye krav. Aftale mellem Regeringen og Dansk Folkeparti*, 7 November 2010, 3, http://www.danskfolkeparti.dk/pictures_org/nye_tider_nye_krav.pdf.

54 Emily Cochran Bech and Per Mouritsen, "Restricting the Right to Family Migration in Denmark: When Human Rights Collide with a Welfare State under Pressure," in *Europe's Immigration Challenge: Reconciling Work, Welfare and Mobility*, ed. Elena Jurado and Grete Brochmann (London: I.B. Taurus, 2013), 159–84.

55 Interview Number 13, Copenhagen, 7 May 2013 (my translation).

56 Banting and Kymlicka, *Multiculturalism and the Welfare State*.

57 Banting, "Transatlantic Convergence?" The Multiculturalism Policy Index for twenty-one countries, together with an explanation of the index, scores for each component of the index, and the documentation on which the score is based, can be accessed at www.queensu.ca/mcp.

58 Koning, "Ethnic and Civic Dealings with Newcomers."

59 Ibid.

60 Marjukka Weide, "Citizen-Making at the Language Centres: Civic Education for Immigrants through the Official Danish Language Tuition," in *The Integration and Protection of Immigrants: Canadian and Scandinavian Critiques*, eds. Paul Van Aerschot and Patricia Daenzer (Burlington, VT: Ashgate, 2014), 85–102, 91.

61 Ministeriet for Børn, Undervisning og Ligestilling, "Beståelsesprocent ved indfødsretsprøven og medborgerskabsprøven," 2012, http://www.uvm.dk/Aktuelt/~/UVM-DK/Content/News/Udd/Voksne/2012/Jan/120105-Bestaaelsesprocent-ved-indfoedsretsproeven-og-medborgerskabsproeven.

62 Eva Ersbøll, "On Trial in Denmark," in *A Re-Definition of Belonging? Language and Integration Tests in Europe*, eds. Ricky van Oers, Eva Ersbøll, and Theodora Kostakopoulou (Leiden: Martinus Nijhoff, 2010), 107–52, 150.

63 Søren Pind, "Ordet skal føre kulturkampen," *Berlingske Tidende*, 12 March 2011, http://www.b.dk/kronikker/ordet-skal-foere-kulturkampen (my translation).

64 Karen Jespersen and Ralf Pittelkow, "De politisk korrekte har udråbt landet til deres store forbillede – Men nu får de en våd klud i ansigtet," *Den Korte Avis*, 2015, http://denkorteavis.dk/2015/det-har-vaeret-de-politisk-korrektes-argument-for-at-indvandring-men-nu-smuldrer-glansbilledet/.

65 Ibid. (my translation).

66 Banting, "Transatlantic Convergence?"

67 Jørgensen, "Understanding the Research–Policy Nexus."

68 Interview Number 12, Copenhagen, 6 May 2013 (my translation).

69 The Prime Minister's Office, "Statsminister Anders Fogh Rasmussens Nytårstale," 2002, http://www.stm.dk/_p_7582.html (my translation).

70 Jørgensen, "Understanding the Research–Policy Nexus."

71 Ibid.

72 Interview Number 11, Copenhagen, 6 May 2013 (my translation).

73 Interview Number 11, Copenhagen, 6 May 2013 ("faglig tung rådgivning" vs. "politisk orientert rådgivning" – my translation).

74 In total, the Think Tank on Integration published eight reports during the 2001–07 period.

75 Interview Number 18, Ottawa, 14 April 2014.

76 Interview Number 23, email, 3 July 2013.

77 Jørgensen, "Understanding the Research–Policy Nexus."

Chapter 4

1 Interview Number 4, Oslo, 10 December 2010 (my translation).

2 Johan P. Olsen, "Norway: Slow Learner – or Another Triumph of the Tortoise?," in Olsen and Peters, *Lessons from Experience*, 180–213.

3 Johan P. Olsen, Paul G. Roness, and Harald Sætren, "Norway: Still Peaceful Coexistence and Revolution in Slow Motion," in *Policy Styles in Western Europe*, ed. Jeremy Richardson (London: George Allen and Unwin, 1982), 47–79.

4 John Logue, "The Welfare State: Victim of Its Success," in *The State*, ed. Stephen R. Graubard (New York: Norton, 1979), 69–88.

5 Anton, "Policy-Making and Political Culture in Sweden," 98.

6 Bernt Krohn Solvang and Joralv Moren, "Partsrepresentasjon i komitéer: Litt om utviklingen over tid," in *Den kollegiale forvaltning: Råd og utvalg i sentraladministrasjonen*, ed. Joralv Moren (Oslo: Universitetsforlaget, 1974), 33–6.

7 David Arter, *The Nordic Parliaments: A Comparative Analysis* (London: Hurst, 1984).

8 Tom Christensen et al., *Forvaltning og politikk* (Oslo: Universitetsforlaget, 2002).

9 Ibid., 138.

10 NOU 2004: 20, "Ny Utlendingslov" (Oslo: Statens forvaltningstjeneste, 2004).

11 St. Innst. nr. 185 (2004–2005): *Innstilling fra Kommunalkomiteen om mangfold gjennom inkludering og deltakelse* (Oslo: Stortinget, 2005), 15 (my translation).

12 Ibid., 15 (my translation).

13 UDI, *Anmodningsvedtak fra Stortinget om forsørgeransvar for herboende referanse ved familieinnvandring for ektefeller (Letter 05/7757-2, 2/9-2005)*, 4 (my translation).

14 St. Innst. nr. 185 (2004–2005), 22 (my translation).

15 NOU 2011: 7, *Velferd og Migrasjon. Den norske modellens framtid* (Oslo: Statens Forvaltningstjeneste, 2011).

16 Koning and Banting, "The Canadian Model of Immigration and Welfare."

17 Interview Number 6, Oslo, 13 December 2010.

18 NOU 2011: 14, *Bedre integrering: Mål, strategier, tiltak* (Oslo: Statens Forvaltningstjeneste, 2011).

19 St. meld. nr. 49 (2003–2004): *Mangfold gjennom inkludering og deltakelse: Ansvar og frihet* (Oslo: Kommunal- og regionaldepartementet, 2004).

20 Interview Number 9, Oslo, 11 October 2012 (my translation).

21 St. meld. nr. 49 (2003–2004), 27 (my italics).

22 Ot. prp. nr. 28 (2002–2003): *Om lov om introduksjonsordning for nyankomne innvandrere (introduksjonsloven)* (Oslo: Kommunal- og regionaldepartementet, 2002).

23 Ot. prp. nr. 41 (2004–2005): *Om lov om norsk statsborgerskap (statsborgerloven)* (Oslo: Kommunal- og regionaldepartementet, 2005).

24 NOU 2000: 32, "Lov om erverv og tap av norsk statsborgerskap (Statsborgerloven)" (Oslo: Statens Forvaltningstjeneste, 2000).

25 Anniken Hagelund and Kaja Reegård, "'Changing Teams': A Participant Perspective on Citizenship Ceremonies," *Citizenship Studies* 15, no. 6–7 (2011): 735–48.

26 Interview Number 9, Oslo, 11 October 2012.
27 It should be mentioned that although the Danish citizenship ceremony does not include an oath of allegiance, applicants for Danish citizenship must declare that they promise faithfulness and loyalty to Denmark and the Danish society, and declare to respect Danish law and fundamental Danish principles of justice on their application forms.
28 Grete Brochmann and Anniken Hagelund, "Norway: The Land of the Golden Mean," in Brochmann and Hagelund, *Immigration Policy and the Scandinavian Welfare State 1945–2010*, 149–224.
29 Ot. prp. nr. 50 (2003–2004): *Om lov om endringer i introduksjonsloven* (Oslo: Kommunal- og regionaldepartementet, 2004).
30 Banting, "Transatlantic Convergence?"
31 OECD, "Key Information on Migration Policy and Migration Statistics by Country."
32 St. meld. nr. 18 (2007–2008): *Arbeidsinnvandring* (Oslo: Arbeids- og inkluderingsdepartementet, 2008).
33 Interview Number 8, Oslo, 9 October 2012.
34 St. meld. nr. 30 (2015–2016): *Fra mottak til arbeidsliv – en effektiv integreringspolitikk* (Oslo: Justis- og beredskapsdepartementet, 2016).
35 Tom Christensen and Per Lægreid, "Organising Immigration Policy: The Unstable Balance between Political Control and Agency Autonomy," *Policy & Politics* 37, no. 2 (2009): 161–77.
36 Interview Number 3, Oslo, 10 December 2010.
37 Interview Number 6, Oslo, 13 December 2010.
38 NOU 2011: 14, *Bedre integrering: Mål, strategier, tiltak*, 49 (my translation).
39 March and Olsen, "Rediscovering Institutions."
40 Interview Number 6, Oslo, 13 December 2010.
41 See Duyvendak and Scholten, "Beyond the Dutch 'Multicultural Model.'"
42 Heikki Holmås, "Se til Canada," *Klassekampen*, 6 October 2006.
43 Kjetil Hegna, "Kanadisk modell gir bedre integrering," *Utrop*, 23 April 2008.
44 Frank Meyer, "Et flerkulturelt samfunn," *Klassekampen*, 20 September 2007.
45 Trygve G. Nordby, "Norsk dumskap om integrering," *Dagbladet*, 5 August 2007, 45.
46 Aksel Braanen Sterri, "Se til Canada: Trudeau gir håp til progressive krefter," *Dagbladet*, 23 December 2015 (my translation), http://www.dagbladet.no/2015/12/23/kultur/meninger/kommentar/trudeau/canada/42498658.
47 Interview Number 10, Oslo, 12 October 2012 (my translation).

48 Interview Number 1, Oslo, 9 December 2010; Interview Number 6, Oslo, 13 December 2010.
49 Kristian Elster, "Vi kommer til å få en asylpolitikk som er blant de strengeste i Europa," *NRK*, 29 December 2015, https://www.nrk.no/norge/_-vi-kommer-til-a-fa-en-asylpolitikk-som-er-blant-de-strengeste-i-europa-1.12724216 (my translation).
50 Government of Norway, "Snr. 15/8555, Høringsnotat – Endringer i Utlendingsloven (Instramninger II)" (Oslo: Justis- og beredskapsdepartementet, 2015).
51 Natanael Waage, "Listhaug Concerned after Several Asylum Proposals Rejected by Parliament," *Norway Today*, 6 June 2016, http://norwaytoday.info/news/listhaug-concerned-parliamentary-asylum-processing/.
52 Website of the Norwegian Embassy to Canada, "Visit from Norway's Minister of Immigration and Integration," http://www.emb-norway.ca/norway_and_canada/News/Visit-from-Norways-Minister-of-Immigration-and-Integration/#.V6iZwq6nwdU.
53 OECD, *International Migration Outlook 2012*.
54 Olsen, "Norway: Slow Learner?"
55 Ibid.
56 Ibid., 210.
57 Interview Number 22, Oslo, 12 May 2015.
58 Ibid.
59 See mandate of the Committee on the Long-Term Consequences of High Immigration: https://www.regjeringen.no/en/dep/jd/organisation/councils-and-committees/tidsbegrensede-styrer-rad-og-utvalg/committee-on-the-long-term-consequences-of-high-immigration/id2468501.

Chapter 5

1 Interview Number 22, Oslo, 12 May 2015.
2 Anton, "Policy-Making and Political Culture in Sweden."
3 Ibid., 98.
4 Rose, *Lesson-Drawing in Public Policy*.
5 Bennett, "How States Utilize Foreign Evidence."
6 David Brian Robertson, "Political Conflict and Lesson-Drawing," *Journal of Public Policy* 11, no. 1 (1991): 55–78, 56–7.
7 David Marsh and Mark Evans, "Policy Transfer: Coming of Age and Learning from the Experience," *Policy Studies* 33, no. 6 (2012): 477–81, 477.

8 Simon Bulmer and Stephen Padgett, "Policy Transfer in the European Union: An Institutionalist Perspective," *British Journal of Political Science* 35, no. 1 (2005): 103–26.
9 Dolowitz and Marsh, "Learning from Abroad," 5.
10 Dolowitz and Marsh, "Who Learns What from Whom."
11 Rose, "What Is Lesson-Drawing?," 3.
12 Olsen, Roness, and Sætren, "Norway: Still Peaceful Coexistence."
13 Anton, "Policy-Making and Political Culture in Sweden."
14 Ibid., 99.
15 Olsen, Roness, and Sætren, "Norway: Still Peaceful Coexistence."
16 Einhorn and Logue, *Modern Welfare States*, 155.
17 Petersen and Lundqvist, *In Experts We Trust*, 20.
18 Robert E. Goodin, Martin Rein, and Michael Moran, "The Public and Its Policies," in *The Oxford Handbook of Public Policy*, ed. Robert E. Goodin, Martin Rein, and Michael Moran (Oxford: Oxford University Press, 2006), 10.
19 Arend Lijphart, *Patterns of Democracy: Government Forms and Performance in Thirty-Six Countries* (New Haven, CT: Yale University Press, 1999).
20 Johan P. Olsen, "Voting, 'Sounding Out,' and the Governance of Modern Organizations," *Acta Sociologica* 15, no. 3 (1972): 267–83.
21 Anton, "Policy-Making and Political Culture in Sweden," 94.
22 Thomas J. Anton, *Administered Politics: Elite Political Culture in Sweden* (Boston: Nijhoff, 1980).
23 David Arter, *Scandinavian Politics Today* (Manchester: Manchester University Press, 2008); Einhorn and Logue, *Modern Welfare States*.
24 Interview Number 11, Copenhagen, 6 May 2013; Interview Number 13, Copenhagen, 7 May 2013.
25 NOU 2011: 7, "Velferd og migrasjon. Den norske modellens framtid," 33 (my translation).
26 NOU 2011: 14, "Bedre integrering: Mål, strategier, tiltak."
27 Interview Number 3, Oslo, 10 December 2010.
28 Interview Number 2, Oslo, 9 December 2010; see also NOU 2004: 20, "Ny Utlendingslov."
29 Arter, *Scandinavian Politics Today*.
30 Interview Number 6, Oslo, 13 December 2010.
31 SOU 2005: 50, "Arbetskraftsinvandring till Sverige - befolkningsutveckling, arbetsmarknad i förändring, internationell utblick."
32 NOU 2011: 7, "Velferd og migrasjon. Den norske modellens framtid."
33 The report on Canada was coauthored by Banting and his student, Edward Koning. See Koning and Banting, "The Canadian Model of Immigration and Welfare."

34 Interview Number 6, Oslo, 13 December 2010.
35 SOU 2002: 13, "Vår anhöriginvandring."
36 Hansen et al., "Udlændinge- og integrationspolitik i syv udvalgte lande - SFI's bidrag til baggrundsrapport fra Tænketanken om udfordringer for integrationsindsatsen i Danmark."
37 Arter, *Scandinavian Politics Today*.
38 Velfærdskommissionen, "Fremtidens velfærd - sådan gør andre lande"; Think Tank on Integration in Denmark, "Immigration and Integration Policies in Denmark and Selected Countries."
39 Hearing list: https://www.regjeringen.no/no/dokumenter/horing-nou-20117-velferds-og-migrasjo/id645936/ (accessed 25 June 2015).
40 Hearing list: https://www.regjeringen.no/no/dokumenter/horing-nou-201114-bedre-integrering/id651072/ (accessed 25 June 2015).
41 Ot. prp. nr. 41 (2004–2005): "Om lov om norsk statsborgerskap (statsborgerloven)."
42 Ibid., 50.
43 Anton, "Policy-Making and Political Culture in Sweden," 94.
44 Strand, "Utvärdering av utskottens och EU-nämndens utrikesresor 2010–2013."
45 Lena Hennel, "Politikernas långresor får kritik," *Svenska Dagbladet*, 8 August 2013, http://www.svd.se/politikernas-langresor-far-kritik.
46 See https://www.stortinget.no/no/Hva-skjer-pa-Stortinget/Reiser-og-besok/Reiser.
47 See http://www.ft.dk/Folketinget/udvalg_delegationer_kommissioner/Rejser.aspx and http://utveckling.riksdagen.se/2014/information-om-utskottens-utrikesresor-nu-tillganglig-i-efterhand/.
48 Interview Number 22, Oslo, 12 May 2015.
49 Dolowitz and Marsh, "Learning from Abroad," 7.

Chapter 6

1 Franklin D. Scott, *The United States and Scandinavia* (Cambridge: Harvard University Press, 1950), 11.
2 For more details on the status of multiculturalism in Canada, Denmark, Norway, and Sweden, see Erin Tolley, "Multiculturalism Policy Index: Immigrant Minority Policies," rev. ed. (revision by Madison Vonk) (Kingston: Queen's University, 2016).
3 Lori Wilkinson, "Labor Market Transitions of Immigrant-Born, Refugee-Born, and Canadian-Born Youth," *Canadian Review of Sociology* 45, no. 2 (2008): 151–76; Soojin Yu, Estelle Ouellet, and Angelyn Warmington,

"Refugee Integration in Canada: A Survey of Empirical Evidence and Existing Services," *Refugee* 24, no. 2 (2007): 17–34.

4 Bevelander and Pendakur, "The Labour Market Integration of Refugee and Family Reunion Immigrants."

5 Triadafilos Triadafilopoulos and Craig Damian Smith, "Introduction," in *Wanted and Welcome? Policies for High Skilled Immigrants in Comparative Perspective*, ed. Triadafilos Triadafilopoulos (New York: Springer, 2013), 1–12.

6 See for instance Kymlicka, "The Canadian Model of Diversity"; Reitz, "The Distinctiveness of Canadian Immigration Experience."

7 Rose, *Lesson-Drawing in Public Policy*; Robertson and Waltman, "The Politics of Policy Borrowing."

8 March and Olsen, "Rediscovering Institutions."

9 Mark Evans and Jonathan Davies, "Understanding Policy Transfer: A Multilevel, Multi-Disciplinary Perspective," *Public Administration* 7, no. 2 (1999): 361–85.

10 See also Daenzer, Aerschot, and Rees, "Integration and the Protection of Immigrants: Canadian-Nordic Comparisons."

11 See mandate of the Committee on the Long-Term Consequences of High Immigration: https://www.regjeringen.no/en/dep/jd/organisation/ councils-and-committees/innstillinger/innstillinger-fra-utvalg/ innstillinger-2017/committee-on-the-long-term-consequences-of-high- immigration/id2468501/.

12 Olsen, "Norway: Slow Learner?," 204.

13 Anniken Hagelund, Hanne C. Kavli, and Kaja Reegård, "Jeg følte det var min dag: Om deltakere og deltakelse i statsborgerseremonier 2006–2008" (Oslo: FAFA, 2009), 10.

14 Ibid.

15 Interview Number 1, Oslo, 9 December 2010 (my translation). The trip to Canada by the Norwegian minister for immigration and integration, Sylvi Listhaug, in June 2016 to study the Canadian private sponsorship program for refugees may suggest that the attitudes towards the private-public management of immigration and integration policy are about to change.

16 Rose, "What Is Lesson-Drawing?," 24.

17 Ibid.

18 Interview Number 17, Stockholm, 23 August 2013.

19 Interview Number 6, Oslo, 13 December 2010.

20 Rose, *Lesson-Drawing in Public Policy*; Bennett, "How States Utilize Foreign Evidence"; Robertson, "Political Conflict and Lesson-Drawing."

21 Petersen and Lundqvist, *In Experts We Trust*.

22 See Dussauge-Laguna, "The Neglected Dimension"; Rich, "Measuring Knowledge Utilization."

23 Carl Marklund, "The Social Laboratory, the Middle Way and the Swedish Model: Three Frames for the Image of Sweden," *Scandinavian Journal of History* 34, no. 3 (2009): 275–6.

24 Trygve Ugland, "Canada as an Inspirational Model: Reforming Scandinavian Immigration and Integration Policies," *Nordic Journal of Migration Research* 4, no. 3 (2014): 144–52.

25 Borevi, "Understanding Swedish Multiculturalism."

26 Karin Borevi, "Dimensions of Citizenship: European Integration Policies from a Scandinavian Perspective," in *Diversity, Inclusion and Citizenship in Scandinavia*, ed. Bo Bengtsson, Per Strömblad, and Ann-Helén Bay (Newcastle: Cambridge Scholars Publishing, 2010), 19–46.

27 Will Kymlicka, *Multicultural Odysseys: Navigating the New International Politics of Diversity*, 1st ed. (Oxford: Oxford University Press, 2007), 157.

28 Borevi, "Understanding Swedish Multiculturalism," 148.

29 OECD, *Settling In: OECD Indicators of Immigrant Integration 2012* (Paris: OECD Publishing, 2012), http://dx.doi.org/10.1787/9789264171534-en.

30 See Kühner, "The Dependent Variable Problem."

31 Stein Kuhnle, "The Scandinavian Welfare State in the 1990s: Challenged but Viable," *West European Politics* 23, no. 2 (2000): 209–28.

32 The European Social Survey (ESS) is an academically driven cross-national survey that has been conducted every two years across Europe since 2001; see http://www.europeansocialsurvey.org.

33 Lithman, "Norwegian Multicultural Debates," 257.

34 Ann-Helén Bay, Henning Finseraas, and Axel West Pedersen, "Welfare Dualism in Two Scandinavian Welfare States: Public Opinion and Party Politics," *West European Politics* 36, no. 1 (2013): 199–220.

35 Ibid.

36 Lenard and Straehle, *Legislated Inequality*.

37 Jenna Hennebry, Janet McLaughlin, and Kerry Preibisch, "Out of the Loop: (In)access to Health Care for Migrant Workers in Canada," *Journal of International Migration and Integration* 17, no. 2 (2016): 521–38.

38 Lenard and Straehle, *Legislated Inequality*, 5.

39 Government of Canada, "Facts and Figures 2014: Immigration Overview – Permanent Residents" (Ottawa: Citizenship and Immigration Canada, 2015), http://www.cic.gc.ca/english/pdf/2014-Facts-Permanent.pdf.

40 UNHCR Global Trends 2014 annexes.

41 Tristin Hopper, "Years the Tories Spent Streamlining Immigration System May Bite Them during Refugee Crisis," *National Post*, 8 September 2015,

http://news.nationalpost.com/news/canada/years-the-tories-spent-streamlining-immigration-system-may-bite-them-during-refugee-crisis; Daniel Schwartz, "Canada's Refugee Acceptance Falls Far Short of Stephen Harper's Claims," *CBC News*, 10 September 2015, http://www.cbc.ca/news/politics/canada-refugees-harper-numbers-accepted-1.3222918.

42 Elin Naurin and Patrick Öhberg, "The Interests of Immigrants First: Can Sweden Maintain Its Generous Refugee Policy and Its Generous Welfare State?," *Inroads: The Canadian Journal of Opinion*, no. 34 (2014): 75–83.

43 Ibid., 76.

44 Reitz, "The Distinctiveness of Canadian Immigration Experience," 520.

45 Elke Winter, "Becoming Canadian: Making Sense of Recent Changes to Citizenship Rules," *IRPP Study*, no. 44 (2014), https://www.questia.com/library/journal/1P3-3264762271/becoming-canadian-making-sense-of-recent-changes.

46 Tom Parry, "Liberals Move to Overhaul Rules on Revoking, Granting Citizenship," *CBC*, 25 February 2016, http://www.cbc.ca/news/politics/john-mccallum-citizenship-act-repeal-bill-1.3463471.

47 Ibid.

48 See for instance Jeffrey G. Reitz, "Closing the Gaps between Skilled Immigration and Canadian Labor Markets: Emerging Issues and Priorities," in Triadafilos Triadafilopoulos, *Wanted and Welcome? Policies for High Skilled Immigrants in Comparative Perspective* (New York: Springer, 2013), 1–12, 147–63.

49 Statistics Canada, "Study: Canada's Immigrant Labour Market," *The Daily*, 10 September 2007, http://www.statcan.gc.ca/daily-quotidien/070910/dq070910a-eng.htm.

50 Tim Rees, "From the Bottom Up: Developing a Community Based Immigration Strategy: A Canadian Case Study," in Van Aerschot and Daenzer, *Integration and Protection of Immigrants*, 33–49.

51 Reitz, "Closing the Gaps."

52 Reitz, "The Distinctiveness of Canadian Immigration Experience," 519.

53 Patricia Daenzer, "Migration, Post Migration Policies, and Social Integration in Canada," in *The Integration and Protection of Immigrants: Canadian and Scandinavian Critiques*, eds. Paul Van Aerschot and Patricia Daenzer (Burlington, VT: Ashgate, 2014), 13–31, 15.

54 Ibid., 14.

55 Kymlicka, "The Canadian Model of Diversity," 70.

56 Kuhnle, "The Scandinavian Welfare State."

57 Hilson, *The Nordic Model*, 111.

58 Einhorn and Logue, *Modern Welfare States*, 254.

59 Bo Rothstein, *Just Institutions Matter: The Moral and Political Logic of the Universal Welfare State* (New York: Cambridge University Press, 1998), 220.
60 Lenard and Straehle, *Legislated Inequality*.
61 Ibid., 11.
62 Ibid., 12.
63 Ibid., 12.
64 Interview Number 10, Oslo, 12 October 2012 (my translation).
65 Lenard and Straehle, *Legislated Inequality*.
66 Ibid.
67 Reitz, "The Distinctiveness of Canadian Immigration Experience."
68 See Employment and Social Development Canada for a full description of the recent reforms to the Temporary Foreign Worker Program: https://www.canada.ca/en/employment-social-development/services/foreign-workers/reports/overhaul.html.
69 Robert Fife, "Temporary Foreign Workers Program Faces Federal Review," *Globe and Mail*, 17 February 2016, http://www.theglobeandmail.com/news/politics/temporary-foreign-workers-program-faces-federal-review/article28792323.
70 Interview Number 8, Oslo, 9 October 2012.
71 Naurin and Öhberg, "The Interests of Immigrants First."
72 Interview Number 15, Stockholm, 19 August 2013.
73 Kymlicka, "Marketing Canadian Pluralism."
74 Kymlicka, "The Canadian Model of Diversity," 64.
75 Wolman, "Understanding Cross National Policy Transfers"; Dolowitz and Marsh, "Who Learns What from Whom."

Bibliography

Abu-Laban, Yasmeen, and Christina Gabriel. *Selling Diversity: Immigration, Multiculturalism, Employment Equity, and Globalization*. Peterborough, ON: Broadview Press, 2002.

Andersen, John, Jørgen Elm Larsen, and Iver Hornemann Møller. "The Exclusion and Marginalisation of Immigrants in the Danish Welfare Society: Dilemmas and Challenges." *International Journal of Sociology and Social Policy* 29, no. 5/6 (2009): 274–86.

Anton, Thomas J. *Administered Politics: Elite Political Culture in Sweden*. Boston, MA: Nijhoff, 1980.

———. "Policy-Making and Political Culture in Sweden." *Scandinavian Political Studies*, no. 4 (1969): 88–102.

Arter, David. *Scandinavian Politics Today*. 2nd ed. Manchester: Manchester University Press, 2008.

———. *The Nordic Parliaments: A Comparative Analysis*. London: Hurst, 1984.

Banting, Keith. "Is There a Progressive's Dilemma in Canada? Immigration, Multiculturalism and the Welfare State." *Canadian Journal of Political Science/ Revue Canadienne de Science Politique* 43, no. 4 (2010): 797–820.

———. "Transatlantic Convergence? The Archaeology of Immigrant Integration in Canada and Europe." *International Journal: Canada's Journal of Global Policy Analysis* 69, no. 1 (2014): 66–84.

Banting, Keith, and Will Kymlicka, eds. *Multiculturalism and the Welfare State: Recognition and Redistribution in Contemporary Democracies*. 1st ed. Oxford: Oxford University Press, 2006.

Bauder, Harald, Patti Tamara Lenard, and Christine Straehle. "Lessons from Canada and Germany: Immigration and Integration Experiences Compared." *Comparative Migration Studies* 2, no. 1 (2014): 1–7.

Bay, Ann-Helén, Henning Finseraas, and Axel West Pedersen. "Welfare Dualism in Two Scandinavian Welfare States: Public Opinion and Party Politics." *West European Politics* 36, no. 1 (2013): 199–220.

Bennett, Colin J. "How States Utilize Foreign Evidence." *Journal of Public Policy* 11, no. 1 (1991): 31–54.

———. "What Is Policy Convergence and What Causes It?" *British Journal of Political Science* 21, no. 2 (1991): 215–33.

Benson, David, and Andrew Jordan. "What Have We Learned from Policy Transfer Research? Dolowitz and Marsh Revisited." *Political Studies Review* 9, no. 3 (2011): 366–78.

Bertossi, Christophe. "National Models of Integration in Europe: A Comparative and Critical Analysis." *American Behavioral Scientist* 55, no. 12 (2011): 1561–80.

Bertossi, Chrisophe, and Jan Willem Duyvendak. "National Models of Integration in Europe: The Costs for Comparative Research." *Comparative European Politics* 10, no. 5 (2012): 237–47.

Bevelander, Pieter, and Ravi Pendakur. "The Labour Market Integration of Refugee and Family Reunion Immigrants: A Comparison of Outcomes in Canada and Sweden." *Journal of Ethnic and Migration Studies* 40, no. 5 (2014): 689–709.

Bissoondath, Neil. *Selling Illusions: The Cult of Multiculturalism in Canada.* Toronto: Penguin Books, 2002.

Borevi, Karin. "Dimensions of Citizenship: European Integration Policies from a Scandinavian Perspective." In *Diversity, Inclusion and Citizenship in Scandinavia*, edited by Bo Bengtsson, Per Strömblad, and Ann-Helén Bay, 19–46. Newcastle: Cambridge Scholars Publishing, 2010.

———. "Sweden: The Flagship of Multiculturalism." In Brochmann and Hagelund, *Immigration Policy and the Scandinavian Welfare State 1945–2010*, 25–96.

———. "Understanding Swedish Multiculturalism." In Kivisto and Wahlbeck, *Debating Multiculturalism in the Nordic Welfare States*, 140–69.

Brochmann, Grete. "Citizens of Multicultural States." In *The Multicultural Challenge*, edited by Grete Brochmann, 1–11. Oxford: Elsevier, 2003.

Brochmann, Grete, and Anne Britt Djuve. "Multiculturalism or Assimilation? The Norwegian Welfare State Approach." In Kivisto and Wahlbeck, *Debating Multiculturalism in the Nordic Welfare States*, 219–45.

Brochmann, Grete, and Anniken Hagelund, eds. *Immigration Policy and the Scandinavian Welfare State 1945–2010.* Houndmills, Basingstoke, Hampshire: Palgrave Macmillan, 2012.

———. "Migrants in the Scandinavian Welfare State." *Nordic Journal of Migration Research* 1, no. 1 (2011): 13–24.

———. "Norway: The Land of the Golden Mean." In Brochmann and Hagelund, *Immigration Policy and the Scandinavian Welfare State 1945–2010*, 149–224.

Brubaker, Rogers. *Citizenship and Nationhood in France and Germany*. Cambridge: Harvard University Press, 1992.

Brunsson, Nils. *The Organization of Hypocrisy: Talk, Decisions and Actions in Organizations*. Chichester: John Wiley & Sons, 1989.

Bulmer, Simon. "Politics in Time Meets the Politics of Time: Historical Institutionalism and the EU Timescape." *Journal of European Public Policy* 16, no. 2 (2009): 307–24.

Bulmer, Simon, and Stephen Padgett. "Policy Transfer in the European Union: An Institutionalist Perspective." *British Journal of Political Science* 35, no. 1 (2005): 103–26.

Cairns, Alan. *Citizens Plus: Aboriginal Peoples and the Canadian State*. Vancouver: UBC Press, 2011.

Childs, Marquis. *Sweden: The Middle Way*. New Haven, CT: Yale University Press, 1936.

Christensen, Tom. "Modern State Reforms." In Heidar, *Nordic Politics*, 24–39.

Christensen, Tom, Morten Egeberg, Helge O. Larsen, Per Lægreid, and Paul G. Roness. *Forvaltning og politikk*. Oslo: Universitetsforlaget, 2002.

Christensen, Tom, and Per Lægreid. "Organising Immigration Policy: The Unstable Balance between Political Control and Agency Autonomy." *Policy & Politics* 37, no. 2 (2009): 161–77.

Christensen, Tom, Per Lægreid, Paul G. Roness, and Kjell A. Røvik. *Organization Theory and the Public Sector: Instrument, Culture and Myth*. London: Routledge, 2007.

Citizenship and Immigration Canada. *CIC Annual Tracking Survey – Winter 2010 Final Report*. Ottawa: Ekos Research, 2010.

Cochran Bech, Emily, and Per Mouritsen. "Restricting the Right to Family Migration in Denmark: When Human Rights Collide with a Welfare State under Pressure." In *Europe's Immigration Challenge: Reconciling Work, Welfare and Mobility*, edited by Elena Jurado and Grete Brochmann, 159–84. London: I.B. Taurus, 2013.

Common, Richard. *Public Management and Policy Transfer in Southeast Asia*. Aldershot: Ashgate, 2001.

Council of Europe. *Report by Mr. Alvaro Gil-Robles, Commissioner for Human Rights, on His Visit to Denmark, 13–16 April 2004*. Strasbourg: Council of Europe, 2004. http://www.refworld.org/docid/41596b8d4.html.

Cuperus, René, Karl Duffek, and Johannes Kandel. *The Challenge of Diversity: European Social Democracy Facing Migration, Integration and Multiculturalism*. Innsbruck: Studien Verlag, 2003.

Daenzer, Patricia. "Migration, Post Migration Policies, and Social Integration in Canada." In *The Integration and Protection of Immigrants: Canadian and Scandinavian Critiques*, edited by Paul Van Aerschot and Patricia Daenzer, 13–31. Burlington, VT: Ashgate, 2014.

Daenzer, Patricia, Paul van Aerschot, and Tim Rees, "Integration and the Protection of Immigrants: Canadian-Nordic Comparisons." In *The Integration and Protection of Immigrants: Canadian and Scandinavian Critiques*, edited by Paul Van Aerschot and Patricia Daenzer, 213–22. Burlington, VT: Ashgate, 2014.

DeVoretz, Don J., Sergiy Pivnenko, and Morton Beiser. "The Economic Experiences of Refugees in Canada." In *Homeland Wanted: Interdisciplinary Perspective on Refugee Settlement in the West*, edited by Peter Waxman and Val Colic-Peisker, 1–21. New York: Nova Science Publishers, 2004.

DiMaggio, Paul J., and Walter W. Powell. "The Iron Cage Revisited: Institutional Isomorphism and Collective Rationality in Organizational Fields." *American Sociological Review* 48 (1983): 147–60.

Dolowitz, David. "Learning by Observing: Surveying the International Arena." *Policy & Politics* 37, no. 3 (2009): 317–34.

Dolowitz, David, and David Marsh. "Learning from Abroad: The Role of Policy Transfer in Contemporary Policy-Making." *Governance* 13, no. 1 (2000): 5–23.

———. "Who Learns What from Whom: A Review of the Policy Transfer Literature." *Political Studies* 44, no. 2 (1996): 343–57.

Dunleavy, Patrick, and Christopher Hood. "From Old Public Administration to New Public Management." *Public Money & Management* 14, no. 3 (1994): 9–16.

Dussauge-Laguna, Mauricio I. "The Neglected Dimension: Bringing Time Back into Cross-National Policy Transfer Studies." *Policy Studies* 33, no. 6 (2012): 567–85.

Duyvendak, Jan Willem, and Peter Scholten. "Beyond the Dutch 'Multicultural Model': The Coproduction of Integration Policy Frames." *Journal of International Migration and Integration* 12 (2011): 331–48.

———. "Deconstructing the Dutch Multicultural Model: A Frame Perspective on Dutch Immigrant Integration Policymaking." *Comparative European Politics* 10, no. 3 (2012): 266–82.

Einhorn, Eric S., and John Logue. *Modern Welfare States: Scandinavian Politics and Policy in the Global Age*. New York: Praeger, 2003.

———. "The Scandinavian Democratic Model." *Scandinavian Political Studies* 9, no. 3 (1986): 193–208.

Elder, Neil, Alastair H Thomas, and David Arter. *The Consensual Democracies?: The Government and Politics of the Scandinavian States*. Oxford and New York: Blackwell, 1988.

Elster, Kristian. "Vi kommer til å få en asylpolitikk som er blant de strengeste i Europa." *NRK*, 29 December 2015. https://www.nrk.no/norge/_-vi-kommer-til-a-fa-en-asylpolitikk-som-er-blant-de-strengeste-i-europa-1.12724216.

Emilsson, Henrik. "Vad kan vi lära av Kanadas migrations- og integrationspolitik?" *Integrationsbloggen* (blog). February 2011. http://integrationsbloggen.blogspot.ca.

Emilsson, Henrik, Karin Magnusson, Sayaka Osanami Törngren, and Pieter Bevelander. *The World's Most Open Country: Labour Migration to Sweden after the 2008 Law*. Malmö: Malmö Institute for Studies of Migration, Diversity and Welfare, Malmö University, 2014.

Entzinger, Han. "The Rise and Fall of Multiculturalism: The Case of the Netherlands." In *Towards Assimilation and Citizenship: Immigrants in Liberal States*, edited by Christian Joppke and Eva Morawska, 59–86. Hampshire: Palgrave, 2003.

Ersbøll, Eva. "On Trial in Denmark." In *A Re-Definition of Belonging? Language and Integration Tests in Europe*, edited by Ricky van Oers, Eva Ersbøll, and Theodora Kostakopoulou, 107–52. Leiden: Martinus Nijhoff, 2010.

Ettelt, Stefanie, Nicholas Mays, and Ellen Nolte. "Policy Learning from Abroad: Why It Is More Difficult than It Seems." *Policy & Politics* 40, no. 4 (2012): 491–504.

Evans, Mark, and Jonathan Davies. "Understanding Policy Transfer: A Multi-level, Multi-disciplinary Perspective." *Public Administration* 7, no. 2 (1999): 361–85.

Fearon, James D. "Ethnic and Cultural Diversity by Country." *Journal of Economic Growth* 8, no. 2 (2003): 195–222.

Fife, Robert. "Temporary Foreign Workers Program Faces Federal Review." *Globe and Mail*, 17 February 2016. http://www.theglobeandmail.com/news/politics/temporary-foreign-workers-program-faces-federal-review/article28792323.

Ford, Richard. *Canada*. New York: Ecco, 2012.

Frank Hansen, Marianne, Marie Louise Schultz-Nielsen, and Torben Tranæs. "The Fiscal Impact of Immigration to Welfare States of the Scandinavian Type." Paper presented at the IZA/Ministry of Finance, Slovak Republic (IFP)/Council for Budget Responsibility (CBR)/CELSI Conference on Fiscal Policy Tools and Labor Markets during the Great Recession, Bratislava, Slovakia, 26–27 October 2015.

Freeman, Gary P. "National Models, Policy Types, and the Politics of Immigration in Liberal Democracies." *West European Politics* 29, no. 2 (2006): 227–47.

Gagnon, Alain-G, and Raffaele Iacovino. *Federalism, Citizenship, and Quebec: Debating Multinationalism*. Toronto and Buffalo: University of Toronto Press, 2007.

———. "Interculturalism: Expanding the Boundaries of Citizenship." In *Democracy, Nationalism and Multiculturalism*, edited by Ramón Máiz and Ferrán Requejo, 25–42. New York: Frank Cass Publishers, 2005.

Goodin, Robert E., Martin Rein, and Michael Moran. "The Public and Its Policies." In *The Oxford Handbook of Public Policy*, edited by Robert E. Goodin, Martin Rein, and Michael Moran, 3–35. Oxford: Oxford University Press, 2006.

Government of Canada. "Annual Report on the Operation of the Canadian Multiculturalism Act 2011–2012: Promoting Integration." Ottawa: Citizenship and Immigration Canada, 2012.

———. "Facts and Figures 2015: Immigration Overview – Permanent Residents." Ottawa: Immigration, Refugees and Citizenship Canada, 2016. http://open.canada.ca/data/en/dataset/2fbb56bd-eae7-4582-af7d-a197d185fc93.

———. "Guide to the Private Sponsorship of Refugees Program." 1 November 2003. http://www.cic.gc.ca/english/resources/publications/ref-sponsor/section-2.asp.

Government of Denmark. *En ny chance til alle: regeringens integrationsplan*. Copenhagen: Ministeriet for Flygtninge, Indvandrere og Integration, 2005.

———. *En ny udlændingepolitik*. Copenhagen: Statsministeriet, 2002.

———. "Nye tider. Nye krav. Aftale mellem Regeringen og Dansk Folkeparti, 7 November 2010." http://www.danskfolkeparti.dk/pictures_org/nye_tider_nye_krav.pdf.

———. *På vej mod en ny integrationspolitik*. Copenhagen: Regeringen, 2002.

———. *Regeringens integrations – og udlændingepolitik – Status Marts 2003*. Copenhagen: Regeringen, 2003.

Government of Norway. "Snr. 15/8555 Høringsnotat – Endringer i Utlendingsloven (Instramninger II)." Oslo: Justis- og beredskapsdepartementet, 2015.

Government of Quebec. Bill 60 – Charter Affirming the Values of State Secularism and Religious Neutrality and of Equality between Women and Men, and Providing a Framework for Accommodation Requests. Quebec: Quebec Official Publisher, 2013.

Government of Scotland. "Scotland's Future: Your Guide to an Independent Scotland." Edinburgh: The Scottish Government, 2013.

Government of Sweden. *"Sweden's Migration and Asylum Policy: Fact Sheet."* February 2017. http://www.government.se/491b3d/contentassets/26536c43ab3b41df90c064c2049b1bce/swedens-migration-and-asylum-policy.

Green-Pedersen, Christoffer, and Jesper Krogstrup. "Immigration as a Political Issue in Denmark and Sweden." *European Journal of Political Research* 47, no. 5 (2008): 610–34.

Griffith, Andrew. *Multiculturalism in Canada: Evidence and Anecdote.* Ottawa: Anar Press, 2015.

Hagelund, Anniken, Hanne C. Kavli, and Kaja Reegård. "Jeg følte det var min dag: Om deltakere og deltakelse i statsborgerseremonier 2006–2008." Oslo: FAFO, 2009.

Hagelund, Anniken, and Kaja Reegård. "'Changing Teams': A Participant Perspective on Citizenship Ceremonies." *Citizenship Studies* 15, no. 6–7 (2011): 735–48.

Hansen, Hans, Garbi Schmidt, Karen Margrethe Dahl, and Sergi Vidal Torre. "Udlændinge- og integrationspolitik i syv udvalgte lande – SFI's bidrag til baggrundsrapport fra Tænketanken om udfordringer for integrationsindsatsen i Danmark." Copenhagen: Danish National Institute of Social Research, 2004.

Hegna, Kjetil. "Kanadisk modell gir bedre integrering." *Utrop*, 23 April 2008.

Heidar, Knut. *Nordic Politics: Comparative Perspectives.* Oslo: Universitetsforlaget, 2004.

Helliwell, John, Richard Layard, and Jeffrey Sachs. *World Happiness Report 2013.* New York: Sustainable Development Solutions Network, 2013.

Hennebry, Jenna, Janet McLaughlin, and Kerry Preibisch. "Out of the Loop: (In)access to Health Care for Migrant Workers in Canada." *Journal of International Migration and Integration* 17, no. 2 (2016): 521–38.

Hennel, Lena. "Politikernas långresor får kritik." *Svenska Dagbladet*, 8 August 2013. http://www.svd.se/politikernas-langresor-far-kritik.

Hilson, Mary. *The Nordic Model: Scandinavia since 1945.* London: Reaktion Books, 2008.

Hoberg, George. "Sleeping with an Elephant: The American Influence on Canadian Environmental Regulation." *Journal of Public Policy* 11, no. 1 (1991): 107–31.

Hojem, Petter, and Martin Ådahl, eds. *Kanadamodellen: Hur invandring leder till jobb.* Stockholm: Fores, 2011.

Holmås, Heikki. "Se til Canada." *Klassekampen*, 6 October 2006.

Hopper, Tristin. "Years the Tories Spent Streamlining Immigration System May Bite Them during Refugee Crisis." *National Post*, 8 September 2015. http://news.nationalpost.com/news/canada/years-the-tories-spent-streamlining-immigration-system-may-bite-them-during-refugee-crisis.

Horváth, Dezsö, and Donald J. Daly. "Small Countries in the World Economy: The Case of Sweden – What Can Canada Learn from the Swedish Experience." Halifax, NS: Institute for Research on Public Policy, 1989.

Howlett, Michael, and Sima Joshi-Koop. "Transnational Learning, Policy Analytical Capacity, and Environmental Policy Convergence: Survey Results from Canada." *Global Environmental Change* 21, no. 1 (2011): 85–92.

Iacovino, Raffaele. "Canadian Federalism and the Governance of Immigration." In *The Politics of Immigration in Multi-Level States*, 86–107. Basingstoke: Palgrave Macmillan, 2014.

Ibbitson, John. "Let Sleeping Dogs Lie." In Stein et al., *Uneasy Partners*, 49–69.

Information. "Et foregangsland." *Information*, 26 January 2002. https://www.information.dk/65291.

Ingebritsen, Christine. *Scandinavia in World Politics*. Lanham: Rowman & Littlefield, 2006.

Irvine, J.A. Sandy. "Canadian Refugee Policy and the Role of International Bureaucratic Networks in Domestic Paradigm Change." In *Policy Paradigms, Transnationalism and Domestic Politics*, edited by Grace Skogstad, 171–201. Toronto: University of Toronto Press, 2011.

Jespersen, Karen, and Ralf Pittelkow. "De politisk korrekte har udråbt landet til deres store forbillede – Men nu får de en våd klud i ansigtet." *Den Korte Avis*, 2015. http://denkorteavis.dk/2015/det-har-vaeret-de-politisk-korrektes-argument-for-at-indvandring-men-nu-smuldrer-glansbilledet/.

Joppke, Christian. *Immigration and the Nation-State: The United States, Germany and Great Britain*. Oxford and New York: Oxford University Press, 1999.

———. "The Retreat of Multiculturalism in the Liberal State: Theory and Policy." *British Journal of Sociology* 55, no. 2 (2004): 237–57.

———. *Selecting by Origin: Ethnic Migration in the Liberal State*. Cambridge, MA: Harvard University Press, 2005.

Jønsson, Heidi Vad, and Klaus Petersen. "Denmark: A National Welfare State Meets the World." In Brochmann and Hagelund, *Immigration Policy and the Scandinavian Welfare State*, 97–148.

Jørgensen, Jakob Stig. "Konservative: Indvandrere skal deles op i gode og dårlige." *Politiken*, 14 November 2013. http://politiken.dk/indland/politik/ECE2131527/konservative-indvandrere-skal-deles-op-i-gode-og-daarlige/.

Jørgensen, Martin Bak. "Understanding the Research–Policy Nexus in Denmark and Sweden: The Field of Migration and Integration." *British Journal of Politics and International Relations* 13, no. 1 (2011): 93–109.

Keating, Michael, and Malcolm Harvey. *Small Nations in a Big World: What Scotland Can Learn?* Edinburgh: Luath Press, 2014.

Kelley, Ninette, and Michael Trebilcock. *The Making of the Mosaic: A History of Canadian Immigration Policy*. 2nd ed. Toronto: University of Toronto Press, 2010.

Kivisto, Peter, and Östen Wahlbeck, eds. *Debating Multicultualism in the Nordic Welfare States*. Basingstoke: Palgrave Macmillan, 2013.

Kjær, Kim U. "The Abolition of the Danish de facto Concept." *International Journal of Refugee Law* 15, no. 2 (2003): 254–75.

Klein, Rudolf. "Learning from Others: Shall the Last Be the First?" *Journal of Health Politics, Policy and Law* 22, no. 5 (1997): 1267–78.

Koning, Edward A. "Ethnic and Civic Dealings with Newcomers: Naturalization Policies and Practices in Twenty-Six Immigration Countries." *Ethnic and Racial Studies* 34, no. 11 (2011): 1974–94.

Koning, Edward A., and Keith Banting. "The Canadian Model of Immigration and Welfare." In NOU, 2011:7 – *Velferd og migrasjon: Den norske modellens framtid*, 354–71, 2011.

Koopmans, Ruud, Paul Statham, Marco Giugni, and Florence Passy. *Contested Citizenship: Immigration and Cultural Diversity in Europe*. Minneapolis: University of Minnesota Press, 2005.

Kuhnle, Stein. "The Scandinavian Welfare State in the 1990s: Challenged but Viable." *West European Politics* 23, no. 2 (2000): 209–28.

Kymlicka, Will. "The Canadian Model of Diversity in a Comparative Perspective." In *Multiculturalism and the Canadian Constitution*, edited by Stephen Tierney, 61–90. Vancouver: UBC Press, 2007.

———. "Disentangling the Debate." In Stein et al., *Uneasy Partners*, 137–56.

———. "Marketing Canadian Pluralism in the International Arena." *International Journal* 59, no. 4 (2004): 829–52.

———. *Multicultural Odysseys: Navigating the New International Politics of Diversity*. 1st ed. Oxford: Oxford University Press, 2007.

Labman, Shauna. "Private Sponsorship: Complementary or Conflicting Interests?" *Refuge: Canada's Journal on Refugees* 32, no. 2 (2016): 67–80.

Laczko, Leslie S. "Canada's Pluralism in Comparative Perspective." *Ethnic and Racial Studies* 17, no. 1 (1994): 20–41.

Lægaard, Sune. "Danish Anti-multiculturalism? The Significance of the Political Framing of Diversity." In Kivisto and Wahlbeck, *Debating Multiculturalism in the Nordic Welfare States*, 170–96.

Lave, Charles A., and James G. March. *An Introduction to Models in Social Sciences*. Lanham, MD: University Press of America, 1993.

Lenard, Patti Tamara, and Christine Straehle. *Legislated Inequality: Temporary Labour Migration in Canada*. Montreal: McGill-Queen's University Press, 2012.

Lijphart, Arend. *Patterns of Democracy: Government Forms and Performance in Thirty-Six Countries*. New Haven, CT: Yale University Press, 1999.

Lisheng, Dong, Tom Christensen, and Martin Painter. "A Case Study of China's Administrative Reform: The Importation of the Super-Department." *American Review of Public Administration* 40, no. 2 (2010): 170–88.

Lithman, Yngve. "Norwegian Multicultural Debates in a Scandinavian Comparative Perspective." In Kivisto and Wahlbeck, *Debating Multiculturalism in the Nordic Welfare States*, 246–69.

Logue, John. "The Welfare State: Victim of Its Success." In *The State*, edited by Stephen R. Graubard, 69–88. New York: Norton, 1979.

Lundqvist, Åsa, and Klaus Petersen, eds. *In Experts We Trust: Knowledge, Politics and Bureaucracy in Nordic Welfare States*. Odense: University Press of Southern Denmark, 2010.

March, James G., and Johan P. Olsen. "The Institutional Dynamics of International Political Orders." *International Organization* 52, no. 4 (1998): 943–69.

———. "The Logic of Appropriateness." In *The Oxford Handbook of Public Policy*, edited by Michael Moran, Martin Rein, and Robert E. Goodin, 689–708. Oxford: Oxford University Press, 2006.

———. *Rediscovering Institutions: The Organizational Basis of Politics*. New York: Free Press, 1989.

Marklund, Carl. "The Social Laboratory, the Middle Way and the Swedish Model: Three Frames for the Image of Sweden." *Scandinavian Journal of History* 34, no. 3 (2009): 264–85.

Marsh, David, and Mark Evans. "Policy Transfer: Coming of Age and Learning from the Experience." *Policy Studies* 33, no. 6 (2012): 477–81.

Martin, Susan F. "International Migration and Global Governance." *Global Summitry* 1, no. 1 (2015): 64–83.

Marwah, Inder, Triadafilos Triadafilopoulos, and Stephen White. "Immigration, Citizenship and Canada's New Conservative Party." In *Conservatism in Canada*, edited by David M. Rayside and James Harold Farney, 95–119. Toronto: University of Toronto Press, 2013.

Mc Andrew, Marie. "Quebec Immigration, Integration and Intercultural Policy: A Critical Assessment." *Indian Journal of Federal Studies* 15, no. 1 (2007): 1–18.

Mc Andrew, Marie, Mathieu Jodoin, Michel Pagé, and Joséfina Rossell. "L'aptitude au français des élèves montréalais d'origine immigrée: impact de la densité ethnique de l'école, du taux de francisation associé à la langue maternelle et de l'ancienneté d'implantation." *Cahiers Québécois de Démographie* 29, no. 1 (2000): 89–117.

Meyer, Frank. "Et flerkulturelt samfunn." *Klassekampen*, 20 September 2007.

Meyer, John. W., and Brian Rowan. "Institutionalized Organizations: Formal Structure as Myth and Ceremony." *American Journal of Sociology* 83, no. 2 (1977): 340–63.

Milner, Henry. "The Prospects for Scandinavian-Style Social Democracy in Quebec/Canada." In *Canada and the Nordic Countries: Proceedings from the Second International Conference of the Nordic Association for Canadian Studies, University of Lund, 1987*, edited by Jørn Carlsen and Bengt Streijfferts, 227–46. Lund: Lund University Press, 1988.

Ministeriet for Børn, Undervisning og Ligestilling. "Beståelsesprocent ved indfødsretsprøven og medborgerskabsprøven," 2012. http://www.uvm.dk/Aktuelt/~/UVM-DK/Content/News/Udd/Voksne/2012/Jan/120105-Bestaaelsesprocent-ved-indfoedsretsproeven-og-medborgerskabsproeven.

Ministry of Employment, Minnesanteckningar från sr Erik Ullenhags resa till USA och Kanada den 18–22 mars 2013. Promemoria A2013/748/IE. Stockholm: Regeringskansliet, 2013.

Mjøset, Lars. "The Nordic Model Never Existed, but Does It Have a Future?" *Scandinavian Studies* 64, no. 4 (1992): 652–71.

Mylenberg, Troels. "Weiss: Arbejde er den bedste integration." *Berlingske*, 21 July 1997.

Naurin, Elin, and Patrick Öhberg. "The Interests of Immigrants First: Can Sweden Maintain Its Generous Refugee Policy and Its Generous Welfare State?" *Inroads: The Canadian Journal of Opinion* Winter/Spring, no. 34 (2014): 75–83.

"The Next Supermodel." *The Economist*, 2 February 2013.

Nielsen, Hans Jørgen. *Er danskerne fremmedfjendske? Udlandets syn på debatten om indvandrerne 2000–2002*. Aarhus: Aarhus Universitetsforlag, 2004.

Nordby, Trygve G. "Norsk dumskap om integrering." *Dagbladet*, 5 August 2007.

NOU 2000: 32. "Lov om erverv og tap av norsk statsborgerskap (Statsborgerloven)." Oslo: Statens Forvaltningstjeneste, 2000.

NOU 2004: 20. "Ny Utlendingslov." Oslo: Statens forvaltningstjeneste, 2004.

NOU 2011: 14. "Bedre integrering: Mål, strategier, tiltak." Oslo: Statens Forvaltningstjeneste, 2011.

NOU 2011: 7. "Velferd og migrasjon. Den norske modellens framtid." Oslo: Statens Forvaltningstjeneste, 2011.

Obinger, Herbert, Carina Schmitt, and Peter Starke. "Policy Diffusion and Policy Transfer in Comparative Welfare State Research." *Social Policy & Administration* 47, no. 1 (2013): 111–29.

OECD. *International Migration Outlook 2012*. Paris: OECD Publishing, 2012. http://dx.doi.org/10.1787/migr_outlook-2012-en.

————. *Settling In: OECD Indicators of Immigrant Integration 2012*. Paris: OECD Publishing, 2012. http://dx.doi.org/10.1787/9789264171534-en.

Olsen, Johan P. "Institutional Design in Democratic Contexts." *Journal of Political Philosophy* 5, no. 3 (1997): 203–29.

————. "Norway: Slow Learner – or Another Triumph of the Tortoise?" In Olsen and Peters, *Lessons from Experience*, 180–213.

————. "Voting, 'Sounding Out,' and the Governance of Modern Organizations." *Acta Sociologica* 15, no. 3 (1972): 267–83.

Olsen, Johan P., and B. Guy Peters. *Lessons from Experience: Experiential Learning in Administrative Reforms in Eight Democracies*. Oslo: Scandinavian University Press, 1996.

Olsen, Johan P., Paul G. Roness, and Harald Sætren. "Norway: Still Peaceful Coexistence and Revolution in Slow Motion." In *Policy Styles in Western Europe*, edited by Jeremy Richardson, 47–79. London: George Allen and Unwin, 1982.

Olwig, Karen Fog, and Karsten Paerregaard. *The Question of Integration: Immigration, Exclusion and the Danish Welfare State*. Newcastle: Cambridge Scholars Publishing, 2011.

Ørtoft, Morten. "Mere målrettet integration på vej." *Aktuelt*, 1997, 1 October edition.

Østergaard-Nielsen, Eva. "Counting the Costs: Denmark's Changing Migration Policies." *International Journal of Urban and Regional Research* 27, no. 2 (2003): 448–54.

Ot.prp. nr. 28 (2002–2003): *Om lov om introduksjonsordning for nyankomne innvandrere (introduksjonsloven)*. Oslo: Kommunal- og regionaldepartementet, 2002.

Ot.prp. nr. 41 (2004–2005): *Om lov om norsk statsborgerskap (statsborgerloven)*. Oslo: Kommunal- og regionaldepartementet, 2005.

Ot.prp. nr. 50 (2003–2004): *Om lov om endringer i introduksjonsloven*. Oslo: Kommunal- og regionaldepartementet, 2004.

Paquin, Stéphane, and Pier-Luc Lévesque. *Social-démocratie 2.0: le Québec comparé aux pays scandinaves*. Montreal: Les Presses de l'Université de Montréal, 2014.

Parry, Tom. "Liberals Move to Overhaul Rules on Revoking, Granting Citizenship." *CBC*, 25 February 2016. http://www.cbc.ca/news/politics/john-mccallum-citizenship-act-repeal-bill-1.3463471.

Peck, Jamie, and Nik Theodore. *Fast Policy: Experimental Statecraft at the Threshold of Neoliberalism*. Minneapolis: University of Minnesota Press, 2015.

Pierson, Paul. *Politics in Time: History, Institutions, and Social Analysis*. Princeton: Princeton University Press, 2004.

Pind, Søren. "Ordet skal føre kulturkampen." *Berlingske Tidende*, 12 March 2011. https://www.b.dk/kronikker/ordet-skal-foere-kulturkampen.

Pollitt, Christopher. *Time, Policy, Management: Governing with the Past*. Oxford: Oxford University Press, 2008.

Poppelaars, Caelesta, and Peter W.A. Scholten. "Two Worlds Apart: The Divergence of National and Local Integration Policies in the Netherlands." *Administration and Society* 40, no. 4 (2008): 335–57.

The Prime Minister's Office. "Statsminister Anders Fogh Rasmussens Nytårstale." 2002. http://www.stm.dk/_p_7582.html.

Proposition 1975/76:26: *Regeringens Proposition om riktlinjer för invandrar- och minoritetspolitiken*. Stockholm: Riksdagen, 1975.

Proposition 1999/2000:147: *Lag om svenskt medborgarskap*. Stockholm: Riksdagen, 2000.

Proposition 2007/08:147: *Nya regler för arbetskraftsinvandring*. Stockholm: Riksdagen, 2008.

Proposition 2009/10:77: *Försörjningskrav vid anhöriginvandring*. Stockholm: Riksdagen, 2010.

Proposition 2013/14:143: *Ett medborgarskap som grundas på samhörighet*. Stockholm: Riksdagen, 2014.

Raynault, Marie-France, Dominique Côté, and Sébastien Chartrand. *Le bon sens à la scandinave: politiques et inégalités sociales de santé*. Montreal: Presses de l'Université de Montréal, 2013.

Rees, Tim. "From the Bottom Up: Developing a Community Based Immigration Strategy: A Canadian Case Study." In *The Integration and Protection of Immigrants: Canadian and Scandinavian Critiques*, edited by Paul Van Aerschot and Patricia Daenzer, 33–49. Burlington, VT: Ashgate, 2014.

Reitz, Jeffrey G. "Closing the Gaps between Skilled Immigration and Canadian Labor Markets: Emerging Issues and Priorities." In *Wanted and Welcome? Policies for High Skilled Immigrants in Comparative Perspective*, edited by Triadafilos Triadafilopoulos, 147–63. New York: Springer, 2013.

———. "The Distinctiveness of Canadian Immigration Experience." *Patterns of Prejudice* 46, no. 5 (2012): 518–38.

Rich, Robert F. "Measuring Knowledge Utilization: Processes and Outcomes." *Knowledge and Policy* 10, no. 3 (1997): 11–24.

Robertson, David Brian. "Political Conflict and Lesson-Drawing." *Journal of Public Policy* 11, no. 1 (1991): 55–78.

Robertson, David Brian, and Jerold L. Waltman. "The Politics of Policy Borrowing." In *Something Borrowed, Something Learned? The Transatlantic Market in Education and Training Reform*, edited by David Finegold, Laurel

McFarland, and William Richardson, 21–44. Washington, DC: Brookings Institution, 1993.

Rochefort, David. A., and Paula Goering. "'More a Link than a Division': How Canada Has Learned from U.S. Mental Health Policy." *Health Affairs* 17, no. 5 (1998): 110–27.

Rokkan, Stein. "Immigranterna och det etablerade partisystemet." In *Identitet och minoritet*, edited by David Schwarz, 209–22. Stockholm: Almqvist & Wiksell, 1971.

Rose, Richard. *Lesson-Drawing in Public Policy: A Guide to Learning across Time and Space*. Chatham: Chatham House Publishers, 1993.

———. "What Is Lesson-Drawing?" *Journal of Public Policy* 11, no. 1 (1991): 3–30.

Rothstein, Bo. *Just Institutions Matter: The Moral and Political Logic of the Universal Welfare State*. New York: Cambridge University Press, 1998.

Runblom, Harald. "Immigration to Scandinavia after World War II." In *Ethnicity and Nation Building in the Nordic World*, edited by Sven Tägil, 282–324. London: Hurst & Company, 1995.

Rytter, Mikkel. "The Family of Denmark and the Aliens: Kinship Images in Danish Integration Policies." In Olwig and Paerregaard, *The Question of Integration*, 54–76.

Sahlin-Andersson, Kerstin. "National, International and Transnational Constructions of New Public Management." In *New Public Management: The Transformation of Ideas and Practice*, edited by Tom Christensen and Per Lægreid, 43–72. Aldershot: Ashgate, 2001.

Schmidke, Oliver. "Beyond National Models? Governing Migration and Integration at the Regional and Local Levels in Canada and Germany." *Comparative Migration Studies* 2, no. 1 (2014): 77–99.

———. "Einwanderungsland Kanada – Ein Vorbild Für Deutschland?" *Aus Politik Und Zeitgeschichte* 44 (2009): 25–32.

Schmidt, Garbi. "Law and Identity: Transnational Arranged Marriages and the Boundaries of Danishness." *Journal of Ethnic and Migration Studies* 37, no. 2 (2011): 257–75.

Schwab, Klaus. *The Global Competitiveness Report 2013–2014: Insight Report*. Geneva: World Economic Forum, 2013.

Schwartz, Daniel. "Canada's Refugee Acceptance Falls Far Short of Stephen Harper's Claims." *CBC News*, 10 September 2015. http://www.cbc.ca/news/politics/canada-refugees-harper-numbers-accepted-1.3222918.

Scott, Franklin D. *The United States and Scandinavia*. Cambridge: Harvard University Press, 1950.

Selznick, Philip. *Leadership in Administration*. New York: Harper & Row, 1957.

Sinclair, Michael. "Canadian Involvement in the Brain Drain from Africa: Opportunities for Action." *Issue: A Journal of Opinion* 9, no. 4 (1979): 19–25.

Solvang, Bernt Krohn, and Joralv Moren. "Partsrepresentasjon i komitéer: Litt om utviklingen over tid." In *Den kollegiale forvaltning: Råd og utvalg i sentraladministrasjonen*, edited by Joralv Moren, 33–6. Oslo: Universitetsforlaget, 1974.

SOU 1997: 162. *Medborgarskap och identitet*. Stockholm: Regeringskanseliet, 1997.

SOU 1999: 34. *Svenskt medborgarskap*. Stockholm: Regeringskanseliet, 1999.

SOU 2002: 13. *Vår anhöriginvandring*. Stockholm: Regeringskanseliet, 2002.

SOU 2005: 50. *Arbetskraftsinvandring till Sverige – befolkningsutveckling, arbetsmarknad i förändring, internationell utblick*. Stockholm: Regeringskanseliet, 2005.

SOU 2006: 87. *Arbetskraftsinvandring till Sverige – förslag och konsekvenser*. Stockholm: Regeringskanseliet, 2006.

SOU 2013: 29. *Det svenska medborgarskapet*. Stockholm: Regeringskanseliet, 2013.

Statistics Canada. "2006 Census: Visible Minority Population and Population Group Reference Guide." 2006. http://www12.statcan.gc.ca/census-recensement/2006/ref/rp-guides/visible_minority-minorites_visibles-eng.cfm.

———. "Definitions, Data Sources and Methods." 2008. http://www.statcan.gc.ca/concepts/index.

———. "Immigration and Ethnocultural Diversity in Canada." National Household Survey, 2011. http://www12.statcan.gc.ca/nhs-enm/2011/as-sa/99-010-x/99-010-x2011001-eng.pdf.

———. "Study: Canada's Immigrant Labour Market." *The Daily*, 10 September 2007. http://www.statcan.gc.ca/daily-quotidien/070910/dq070910a-eng.htm.

Stein, Janice Gross, David Robertson Cameron, John Ibbitson, Will Kymlicka, John Meisel, Haroon Siddiqui, and Michael Valpy. *Uneasy Partners: Multiculturalism and Rights in Canada*. Waterloo, ON: Wilfrid Laurier University Press, 2007.

Sterri, Aksel Braanen. "Se til Canada: Trudeau gir håp til progressive krefter." *Dagbladet*, 23 December 2015. http://www.dagbladet.no/2015/12/23/kultur/meninger/kommentar/trudeau/canada/42498658.

St. Innst. Nr. 185 (2004–2005). *Innstilling fra Kommunalkomiteen om mangfold gjennom inkludering og deltakelse*. Oslo: Stortinget, 2005.

St. meld. Nr. 18 (2007–2008). *Arbeidsinnvandring*. Oslo: Arbeids- og inkluderingsdepartementet, 2008.

————. Nr. 49 (2003–2004). *Mangfold gjennom inkludering og deltakelse: Ansvar og frihet*. Oslo: Kommunal- og regionaldepartementet, 2004.

————. Nr. 30 (2015–2016). *Fra mottak til arbeidsliv – en effektiv integreringspolitikk*. Oslo: Justis- og beredskapsdepartementet, 2016.

Stone, Diane. "Learning Lessons and Transferring Policy across Time, Space and Disciplines." *Politics* 19, no. 1 (1999): 51–9.

Strand, Peter. "Utvärdering av utskottens och EU-nämndens utrikesresor 2010–2013." Stockholm: Utskottsavdelingen, Utvärderings- och forskningssekretariatet, Sveriges Riksdag, 2013.

Strode, Hudson. *Sweden: Model for a World*. New York: Harcourt, Brace, 1949.

"Sweden Slams Shut Its Open-Door Policy towards Refugees." *Guardian*, 24 November 2015. http://www.theguardian.com/world/2015/nov/24/sweden-asylum-seekers-refugees-policy-reversal.

Svensk författningssamling 2008: 567. *Diskrimineringslag*. Stockholm: Sveriges Riksdag, 2008. http://www.riksdagen.se/sv/Dokument-Lagar/Lagar/Svenskforfattningssamling/Diskrimineringslag-2008567_sfs-2008-567/.

Sveriges Riksdag. *Rapport från tredje vice talmansresa till Kanada 31 januari–4 februari 2011, PM 2011 02 10*. Stockholm: Sveriges Riksdag, 2011.

Tænketanken om udfordringer for integrationsindsatsen i Danmark. *Udlændinge- og integrationspolitikken i Danmark og udvalgte lande*. Copenhagen: Ministeriet for Flygtninge, Indvandrere og Integration, 2004.

Taylor, Adam. "A Danish Politician Explains Why It's Okay to Take Valuables from Refugees." *Washington Post*, 27 January 2016. https://www.washingtonpost.com/news/worldviews/wp/2016/01/27/a-danish-politician-explains-why-its-okay-to-take-valuables-from-refugees.

Think Tank on Integration in Denmark. *Immigration and Integration Policies in Denmark and Selected Countries*. Copenhagen: Ministry of Refugee, Immigration and Integration Affairs, 2004.

Tierney, Stephen J. "Introduction: Constitution Building in a Multicultural State." In *Multiculturalism and the Canadian Constitution*, edited by Stephen Tierney, 3–23. Vancouver: UBC Press, 2007.

Tolley, Erin. *Multiculturalism Policy Index: Immigrant Minority Policies*. Rev. ed. (revision by Madison Vonk). Kingston: Queen's University, 2016.

Triadafilopoulos, Triadafilos. "A Model for Europe? A Critical Appraisal of Canadian Integration Policies." In *Politische Steuerung von Integrationsprozessen*, edited by Karen Schönwälder, Sigrid Baringhorst, and Uwe Hunger, 79–94. Wiesbaden: Verlag für Sozialwissenschaften, 2006.

Triadafilopoulos, Triadafilos, and Craig Damian Smith. "Introduction." In *Wanted and Welcome? Policies for High Skilled Immigrants in Comparative*

Perspective, edited by Triadafilos Triadafilopoulos, 1–13. New York: Springer, 2013.

UDI. *Anmodningsvedtak fra Stortinget om forsørgeransvar for herboende referanse ved familieinnvandring for ektefeller (Letter Ref 05/7757-2)*, 2005.

Ugland, Trygve. "Canada as an Inspirational Model: Reforming Scandinavian Immigration and Integration Policies." *Nordic Journal of Migration Research* 4, no. 3 (2014): 144–52.

———. "The Quebec Charter of Values: A Solution in Search of Problems." *Journal of Eastern Townships Studies* 42 (2014): 11–21.

Vatne Pettersen, Silje, and Lars Østby. "Skandinavisk komparativ statistikk om integrering: Innvandrere i Norge, Sverige og Danmark." *Samfunnsspeilet*, no. 5 (2013): 76–82.

Velfærdskommissionen. *Fremtidens velfærd – sådan gør andre lande*. Copenhagen: Velfærdskommissionen, 2005.

———. *Fremtidens velfærd – vores valg*. Copenhagen: Velfærdskommissionen, 2005.

Waage, Natanael. "Listhaug Concerned after Several Asylum Proposals Rejected by Parliament." *Norway Today*, 6 June 2016. http://norwaytoday. info/news/listhaug-concerned-parliamentary-asylum-processing/.

Weide, Marjukka. "Citizen-Making at the Language Centres: Civic Education for Immigrants through the Official Danish Language Tuition." In *The Integration and Protection of Immigrants: Canadian and Scandinavian Critiques*, edited by Paul Van Aerschot and Patricia Daenzer, 85–102. Burlington, VT: Ashgate, 2014.

Westney, Eleanor D. *Imitation and Innovation: The Transfer of Western Organizational Patterns to Meiji Japan*. Cambridge: Harvard University Press, 1987.

Wickström, Mats. "Conceptual Change in Postwar Sweden: The Marginalization of Assimilation and the Introduction of Integration." In Kivisto and Wahlbeck, *Debating Multiculturalism in the Nordic Welfare States*, 110–39.

———. "The Difference White Ethnics Made: The Multiculturalist Turn of Sweden in Comparison to the Cases of Canada and Denmark." In *Migrations and Welfare States: Policies, Discourses and Institutions*, edited by Heidi Vad Jønsson, Saara Pellander, Elizabeth Onasch, and Mats Wickström, 25–58. Helsinki: NordWel, 2013.

Wilkinson, Lori. "Labor Market Transitions of Immigrant-Born, Refugee-Born, and Canadian-Born Youth." *Canadian Review of Sociology* 45, no. 2 (2008): 151–76.

Winter, Elke. "Becoming Canadian: Making Sense of Recent Changes to Citizenship Rules." *IRPP Study*, no. 44 (2014). https://www.questia.com/ library/journal/1P3-3264762271/becoming-canadian-making-sense-of-recent-changes.

———. "Traditions of Nationhood or Political Conjuncture? Debating Citizenship in Canada and Germany." *Comparative Migration Studies* 2, no. 1 (2014): 29–55.

Wolman, Harold. "Understanding Cross National Policy Transfers: The Case of Britain and the US." *Governance* 5, no. 1 (1992): 27–45.

Woodsworth, J.S. *Strangers within Our Gates: Or, Coming Canadians.* Toronto: F.C. Stephenson, 1909.

Yu, Soojin, Estelle Ouellet, and Angelyn Warmington. "Refugee Integration in Canada: A Survey of Empirical Evidence and Existing Services." *Refugee* 24, no. 2 (2007): 17–34.

Index